Leadership

in

Practice

Paul Murtagh

First published 2013

www.paulmurtaghmentor.com

ISBN 978-1 49274 299 9

Contents

Acknowledgements

I am hugely indebted to my family, friends and colleagues, who have constantly supported me in my life and my career.

I could never have achieved anything without you.

About the author

Paul Murtagh was born in 1959 in Dublin, Ireland.

Paul has spent the majority of his career in Information and Communications Technology. Starting in 1979 as a Computer Programmer, Paul went on to start a computer software business in partnership in 1988.

In 1996, Paul joined a large U.S. multinational financial services organization and from 2002 to 2010 was Senior Vice President and Managing Director of their IT and R&D facility in Ireland.

Paul decided to retire in 2011 and is now a mentor and business consultant to start-up businesses.

He is married with three children and holds a Masters in Business Administration (MBA) from the Open University in the U.K. (2000).

Introduction

Leadership is fundamental to developing the human race and in the modern era, leadership plays a central role in our efforts to advance further.

Achievements in all parts of civilisation have their origins in the aspirations of people who feel they have a great idea for advancement.

Leadership is fundamentally about an ambition to make things better and the actualisation of such dreams.

For my own part, I base my thoughts on leadership on two key aspects of my life and I view these with equal importance:

1. *My own personal experience as a leader*

2. *My observations of how other leaders have behaved*

I was fortunate enough to have had a career in which I had a leadership role in a large multinational corporation. By way of real contrast, I was also a partner in a small technology business for a number of years. During this time I learned a great deal about my own capacity to be a leader and as often is the case, I learnt most through the experience of success and mistakes. I also watched others closely and learnt from them and it is perhaps this skill of observation and analysis that gave me a complete insight into leadership.

I spent more days than I care to remember at management off-sites and think-ins and whatever form of group learning and therapy that helps us all do things better.

But I believe in simplicity. And all the lectures and books you read on leadership will not add up to a spoonful of coffee beans if you do not have the fundamental characteristics to be a leader coupled with the ability to learn and develop.

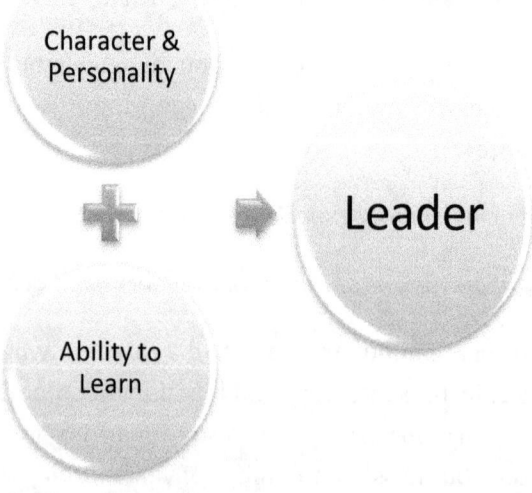

Almost every book you read on leadership will have a Vision as its central theme. This one is no different. Leaders focus on a future state that they believe is better than the current state – this is the *Vision*.

But achieving that future state requires a *Design* on how to get there and the actual *Implementation* of a plan.

We mostly tend to see leaders as people who have vision. And rightly so, because first and foremost, there must be a *Visionary Leader*. And while it is possible that the Visionary leader possesses the necessary design and implementation skills, this is not always the case.

Leaders must fully understand their own capability and then pull together a *Leadership Team* who collectively have the full complement of leadership skills – Vision, Design and Implementation.

The first part of this book will explore a framework for leadership, expressed in terms of the Vision, the Design and the Implementation. It will help you understand your own leadership skills and identify where you fit in the leadership team. It is also about developing your skills as a leader through tuition, coaching, mentoring and experience.

Success is measured by the achievement of a Vision and it is better to be a small cog in a successful team than any cog in a team that fails.

I cannot emphasise enough that a leader must be honest. Look in the mirror and truly accept and understand who you are and what you are capable of. Hopefully this book will take the place of that mirror and help you avoid the state of delusion that is the enemy of leaders and organizations.

Once you know yourself, you can position yourself and others as part of the leadership team. I cannot think of many leaders who brought an organization to a better place single-handed. Leadership can be the loneliest place to be in the most crowded of environments, but the only way to succeed is with the help of others and a good leader never forgets this.

This book will also look at a number of characteristics associated with leaders and how you can grow and develop your leadership ability.

1. There are no perfect leaders

Leadership is about the pursuit of a better place for an organization. But such are the frailties of human nature that absolute perfection in leadership is not possible. There are many aspects of human endeavour in which it is appropriate to speak of the *pursuit* of perfection, but not about the achievement of perfection itself. After all, if one were to attain perfection, there would be nothing left for those who come after us. We must always keep our focus on the *quest* because it is this that enables progress and brings gratification.

The goal of leaders is to bring an organization forward. To develop and improve on where we are today – that is possible. In fact, it is essential. An organization does not stand still. It is either moving forward or dying.

And good leaders bring an organization forward.

So firstly and most important of all is to understand the principal leadership roles. These are the only leadership roles that an organization needs to be successful and all three are fundamental in making an organization develop and survive.

1	**Leader as Visionary**
2	**Leader as Designer**
3	**Leader as Implementer**

The *Visionary Leader* is typically the <u>Organizational Leader</u>. This leader creates the vision of the *future state* and without this vision, an organization has no real direction or purpose.

This book will look at the qualities and skills required to be a successful leader and point to the different skills and capabilities for the visionary, designer and implementer.

As I outline the skills it is important to remember that a leader must have a significantly high level of skill in all these areas. Gaps in your capability will be easily exposed and cause your tenure as a leader to come to an end – quickly.

Because we are all different, it must be acknowledged that every leader will possess these skills to a greater or lesser extent. Leaders should primarily focus on building a leadership team which collectively possesses the full complement of skills.

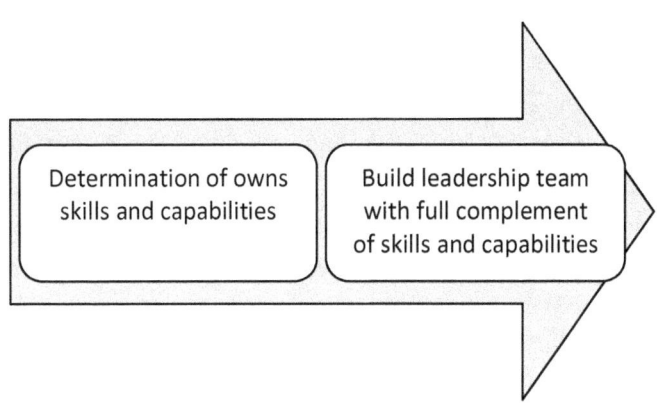

If you cannot assess yourself and others in an honest and realistic way then you run the risk of deluding yourself and others that you are a leader. Ultimately you will lose the most sought-after personal achievement of a leader – respect.

Leaders can develop their capability over time. They get tuition in schools on different models and concepts. They get coached about leadership technique in given circumstances. They can be mentored by successful leaders with extensive experience and learn how to manage their behaviours. And they can experience leadership at first hand. All of which enable a leader to be better at what they do.

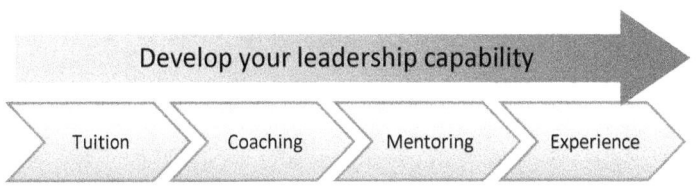

This book is not specifically about leaders in a given area of society. That said, leadership is most visible in the media in specific areas such as business, politics, science, medicine, engineering, human rights, and so on. But we can equally look at leadership at the level of local society, which might include your golf club, parish council, children's sports group, and so on. Regardless, I strongly believe that leadership is a capability that can be applied in many ways and the reason why a leader chooses one field versus another is probably because of their educational background, their personal interests, or the things that influenced them when they were growing up.

Time is the true evaluation of a leader. After many years have passed the legacy of a leader should still be talked about or be evident in what we see and do. Take a trip to many of the capital cities around Europe and you can still see the evidence of leadership that the Roman emperors left behind.

The model of Vision, Design and Implementation may not be immediately obvious in many organizations in society or business. But close examination of leadership in practice will reveal the three roles.

Let's look at some fairly clear examples:

Organization	Vision	Design/Strategy	Implementation
Government	Prime Minister, President	Departmental Ministers	Heads of Government Departments
Sports Team	Owner	Coach/Manager	Captain of Team
Business	Owners	Managing Director	Leadership Team
Charity	Trustees	Managing Director	Leadership Team

The exploration of space is one of the best examples of leadership in recent times and it is clear to see the three types of leadership in action: President John F. Kennedy creates the vision to put a man on the Moon, NASA figures out the strategy to get there and the astronauts actually make the journey. Subsequent leaders built on the achievement by having a vision for a reusable space vehicle (the shuttle) and an International Space Station.

Take some time to look at how your own organization is structured and see if you can identify where Vision, Design and Implementation takes place. Try to identify the leaders in this areas and look closely at your own role as a leader.

2. *Survive, progress, protect*

The human race is pre-programmed to survive and evolve. This is built into our DNA and we share this in common with all living things. Survival is built on the protection of what we have achieved and figuring out what future state will give us the best chance of surviving over the longer term.

Survival means that leaders constantly look for new visions which will continue to develop an organization.

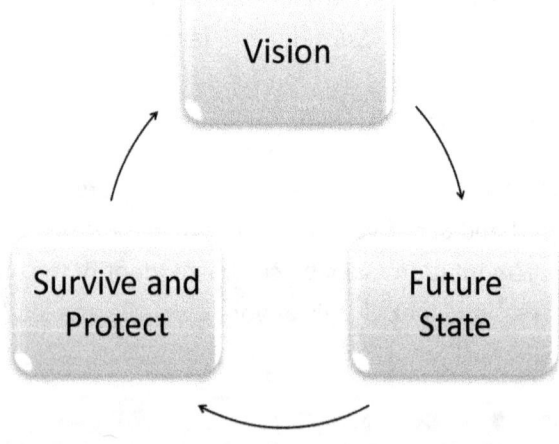

This instinct to survive and develop is a central theme in understanding the function of leadership.

Leaders define a future state which they believe will give the organization the optimum chances of survival and progression.

So if the instinct to survive is built into every human being then why aren't we all leaders? The truth is that very few people become leaders because few people have the ability to create a vision of the 'future state'. For most people, their instinct to survive manifests itself in the perception that it is probably better to follow someone else's path than to try and create your own. We gravitate towards those visions of the future where we feel our personal security and comfort is sustainable. We also feel secure in our survival if a large number of other people believe in the same future state.

Although there have been many great achievements by humans over the course of history, none of them would have been realised without a vision, a strategy to get there and someone willing to make the journey.

Leadership is the most important asset to have when an organization is in the early stages of development. Most of the leaders that you call to mind were key players at organizational beginnings or reinventions. Leaders who maintain the 'steady state' do not share the same level of respect. But in the modern world, the rate at which all things change has increased significantly when compared with, say, 50 or 100 years ago. If an organization develops a new and innovative product, it will only have a limited time before it will need to be improved or replaced; think about how many versions of your computer or phone have been launched in the past three years. So 'steady state' leadership is more or less obsolete and leaders must have the ability to constantly develop, design and implement a new vision on a recurring basis. When the current vision is being implemented, the next one should be in design.

Without that initial vision, nobody knows where we are going and there is no point in setting out on a journey. So it is typical that when we talk about leadership, we tend to focus on the 'Visionary Leaders'.

Visionary leaders have the inspiration to see the benefit that a future state can bring. But they may not have the ability to get there themselves and so they depend on the abilities of others to design strategies and implement roadmaps.

If a Leader cannot get to the future state through their own means, then they need to have powers of influence to convince others to help them.

What is unquestionable is that all leaders understand the vision of a future state. Leaders are convinced that the future state is a better place to be than the current state. For them, the future state represents 'progress'. They behave with confidence and certainty and until the future state is reached and evaluated, they remain convinced.

The risk of failure in leadership, however, is very high. First, we may never get to the future state. Unforeseen obstacles wait around every turn. And if the future state is never reached, we can mistakenly conclude that the 'Visionary

Leader' has failed. This is not true. Until we reach the future state, we cannot really determine if it is a better place to be.

Failure to reach the future state can often result from poor design and implementation. Design and Implementation leaders run significant risk of failure in their endeavours. Once the vision of a future state has been defined, there are bound to be multiple designs to achieve the vision and there are likely to be multiple paths to reach the future state. Choosing the right design and the right path is the core skill of Design and Implementation leaders.

Christopher Columbus had a vision to reach Asia by travelling west. This aspect of his leadership can never be faulted – he had a vision, a good one. So he convinces powerful people to support him – because he does not have all the resources himself. And then he figures out how to get there using navigation by the stars and this constitutes his design (he even has an idea of how long the journey will be). And, finally, he embarks on the journey himself, discovers the 'New World' and is hailed as a great leader. But the risks were enormous.

Columbus was a Visionary leader. But he also took on the role of Design leader by figuring out the way to navigate. Furthermore, he took on the role of Implementation leader by actually captaining the ships that travelled to the 'New World'. And he did not stop there, because he wanted the role of Administration leader in the New World itself!

Columbus took many risks in regard to his leadership. Despite his vision, he might have failed as a Design leader if he sailed in the wrong direction. Equally he could have failed as an Implementation leader if he did not select a good crew or sailed with inadequate supplies. The irony for Columbus is that many regarded him as a failure because he did not discover the mainland. In addition, having found the 'New World' he did not necessarily build on this achievement and again, many regarded him as a failure because he lacked the administration skills necessary to take charge of the day-to-day management of the 'New World'.

Because Columbus was involved in all three levels of leadership, the risk to his success as a leader was constantly tested in terms of 1) His vision – was this a better way to reach Asia? 2) His design – could he map the route? 3) His implementation – could he successfully navigate and lead three ships across a great expanse of ocean?

So how do we characterize 'failure' in leadership?

1. The future state is not reached because we went about it the wrong way (Implementation failure).

2. The future state is not reached because the path we took is ineffective or inefficient (Design failure)

3. The future state is reached but does not represent progress (Visionary failure). It may even represent a step backwards.

If a future state is reached and it is a better place, then it has to be protected and developed. The organization must have sufficient remaining resources to ensure that sustainability and progress is possible. Otherwise it will be lost, and in this way a successful leader can turn into a failure in a very short time. Some leaders bring us to the future state and then stand aside to let another leader figure out how to protect and develop it.

Leaders have tenure and it can last from days to years. But tenure implies an end. To outstay your tenure has the potential to damage your reputation as a leader and can sometimes negate your achievements. Leaders are remembered for their achievements but also for the manner of their exit.

When a leader's tenure comes to an end the manner in which they exit is key to their legacy:

1. The Champion. The vision is reached and it is a better place to be.

2. The Hero. The leader makes great personal sacrifice – regardless of whether the goal is reached.

3. The Shame. The goal is not reached or the goal is reached and it is not a better place. The goal is reached and the leader lacks the ability and/or support to achieve the next vision – but tries nonetheless.

3.   *What a leader needs*

To be a leader requires that you have some key characteristics. These are 'must haves' and are not negotiable. Everyone is born with certain characteristics, but key life events will probably cause some of your characteristics to change. It is essential to understand how the dynamics of change impact your character. It can be useful to read the biographies of leaders and see how key events in their lives impacted their character. Your character is central to determining how you behave towards other people and such behaviours are key to inspiring and influencing others.

Furthermore, a leader needs to build their capability by acquiring skills, knowledge and behavioural techniques. This development will be enabled through education and actual experience as a leader with an organization.

Think of it this way: part of your ability to be a leader comes from the characteristics of you as a person and the balance comes from development of your skills through experience and knowledge.

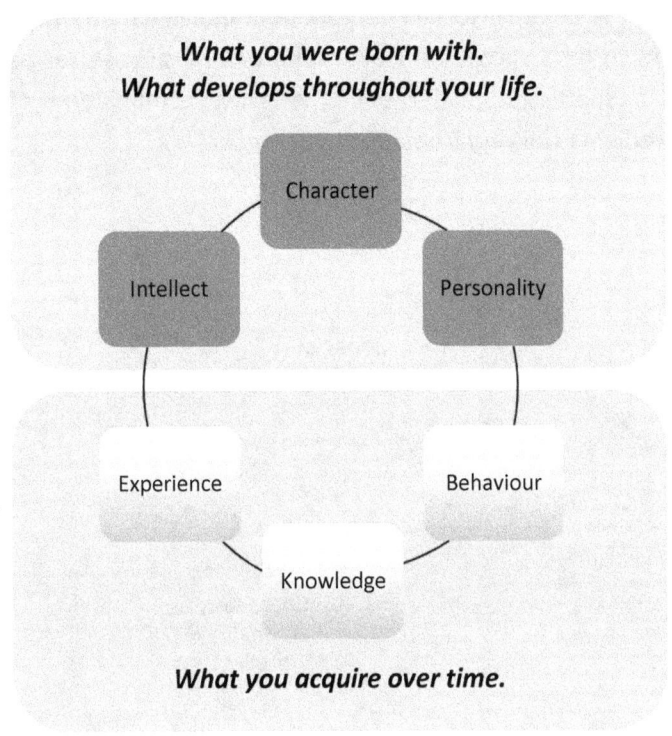

What you were born with.
What develops throughout your life.

Character

Intellect

Personality

Experience

Behaviour

Knowledge

What you acquire over time.

The extent to which leadership skills are derived from you as an individual will vary from person to person. Some people are regarded as 'natural-born leaders', which implies that almost everything about their leadership comes from their character, personality and intellect.

In contrast, many leaders have significantly enhanced their leadership ability through knowledge and experience.

What is certain is that a leader is not exclusively derived from their character, personality and intellect any more than it is possible to take any random individual and train them to be a successful leader. There is no precise recipe for a successful leader and the exact combination of ingredients will vary from person to person.

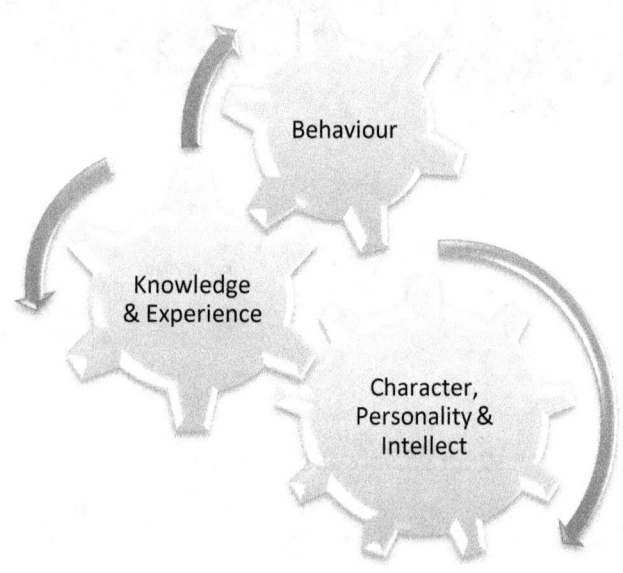

Leadership can be 'hit and miss' and many organizations and governments are testament to this.

In the end, few people become leaders. People who possess the appropriate mix of abilities are not common. What is important is that we understand the qualities that make a person a leader and evaluate our ability in each of these areas.

The characteristics required by a leader depend on the type of leader you are. The Visionary leader must have the inspiration to create a picture of the future state. One of the most outstanding examples of this was the Reverend Martin Luther King Junior, who actually stated, "I have a Dream" and went on to fully describe what that future state looked like.

By comparison, the Design leader needs to determine which path is the most efficient and effective way to reach the future state. Choosing the strategy that makes use of the available resources is a key skill of the Design leader.

And finally the Implementation leader must make the journey and bring the organization to the future state – on time, on budget and in a fit state to survive and protect what has been achieved.

So let's look at the core capabilities required by a leader and show the strength of each one required.

Visionary Leader

Inspiration and Destiny	Critical to success. Ability to define the future state.
Intuition and Judgement	Critical to success. Ability to 'sense' what/who will bring about a successful outcome.
Pick the Right People	Critical to success. Visionary leaders need the help of others to achieve the future state.
Influence	Critical to success. Ability to convince others is essential as support is usually required by sponsors.
Innovation	Medium to high ability. If this leader is not innovative, they can get someone else who is – usually the designer.
Confidence and Certainty	Critical to success. Must constantly revalidate that the goal is achievable and have unwavering undoubting self-belief.
Know yourself	Critical to Success. Understanding what you have and more importantly, what you have not.
Know when to step down	High. There is always a time to let others take over and a Leader must know when.

Design Leader

Inspiration & Destiny	High ability. Does not necessarily define the future state but must be able to understand it fully and outline missions to get there.
Intuition & Judgement	High ability. Must be applied to the design and the consequences of getting it wrong are fatal.
Pick the Right People	Critical to success. Design leaders typically work in a team.
Influence	Moderate ability.
Innovation	Critical to success. This is the key skill of the Design leader in utilizing available resources.
Confidence and Certainty	High ability. Must be convinced that the design will work and dynamically change it where necessary.
Know yourself	High ability. Understanding what you have and more importantly what you have not.
Know when to step down	High ability. If a Design leader cannot get the job done, they must step aside and let someone else take over.

Implementation Leader

Inspiration and Destiny	High ability. Does not necessarily define the future state but must be able to understand it fully.
Intuition and Judgement	High ability. Must be applied at all times throughout the journey and the consequences of getting it wrong are fatal.
Pick the Right People	Critical to success. Implementation leaders typically work in a team.
Influence	Moderate ability.
Innovation	High ability. Getting around the many obstacles is a key characteristic of the Implementation leader.
Confidence and Certainty	High ability. Must be convinced that the process will work and change it where necessary.
Know yourself	High ability. Understanding what you have and more importantly what you have not.
Know when to step down	High ability. If an Implementation leader cannot get the job done, they must step aside and let someone else take over.

Most organizations are led by a team and it is critical that the team has the right balance of leadership at the vision, design and implementation levels. Too many visionaries will argue among themselves about whose vision is right, and unless there are designers and implementers, the organization will go nowhere.

It is clear from the above tables that the Visionary leader needs to have the highest skill level across the characteristics. Again, it is for this reason that the Visionary leader is typically the Organizational leader.

It is a key role of the Organization leader to select the members of the team that will ensure all the necessary leadership skills are present in suitable quantities and with the right balance.

4.   Can I be more than one type of leader?

Yes. And you probably are.

It is entirely possible that Visionary leaders can also be Design leaders and even Implementation leaders. As mentioned, it would appear that Christopher Columbus possessed the skills of all three types of leader. That said, it has been my observation that there are probably four main classifications of leaders:

> 1. Outright Visionaries

> 2. Visionary-Designers

> 3. Designer-Implementers

> 4. End-to-End Leaders - capable of Vision, Design and Implementation

Good examples of outright Visionaries would be President John F. Kennedy, Martin Luther King, Abraham Lincoln and Mao Tse Tung. The key thing that a Visionary leader is renowned for is *inspiration*. They are inspired to bring an organization forward and inspire others to follow them.

By contrast, the most common type of leader is the Visionary-Designer. Not only does this leader know what the future state looks like, but they know how to get there. They surround themselves with strong Implementers and have excellent people management skills. Good examples of visionary-designers would be Bill Gates, Steve Jobs and Winston Churchill.

Designer-Implementers work really well with outright Visionaries. They 'get the job done' by combining their skills of strategic design with their organizational management skills to implement the roadmap to achieve the future state.

End-to-end leaders have the ability to define a vision, develop a strategy and, finally, lead the organization to success by implementing a plan. End-to-end leaders still need to build a leadership team and cannot act as a standalone leader for an organization. Good examples of end-to-end leaders would be Christopher Columbus and Roald Amundsen.

The leader of an organization has the responsibility of ensuring there is harmony within the team. Equally, the Organizational leader has the responsibility to manage conflict between individuals on the team. Understanding the profile of each member of the team can be useful in this process. For example, there is potential for conflict when there are two outright visionaries on a team, each with very strong but different views of the future state.

27

5.   *Inspiration and destiny*

It is not easy to describe sources of inspiration and there have been many stories about how it has impacted the progress of the human race. One that comes to mind is Sir Isaac Newton, who is said to have been inspired to develop his theory of gravity by watching an apple fall from a tree in his garden. Whether this is true or not, there is no doubt that certain <u>events and circumstances</u> stimulate leaders to create the vision of a future state. Visionary leaders are constantly scanning their environment to seek that stimulation. They see things that most people do not see and it triggers an avalanche of ideas which are processed at lightning speed to form an early outline of the future state.

While Visionary leaders do recognise obstacles, it is not unusual for a Visionary leader to quickly dismiss any attempts to block the path to success. What is happening here is that the Visionary leader is focusing in a single-minded way on the vision and feels that overcoming the obstacles is something that will happen at the design and implementation phase. That said, a Visionary leader will constantly validate and re-validate the vision.

The formation of a visionary future state takes time, even if it appears that there has been some 'eureka' moment. The vision needs to be looked at from many angles. Really good Visionary leaders have the ability to identify weaknesses and modify the vision. It is during this phase that confidence grows and certainty sets in. The more tests that a leader subjects their vision to, the more they creatively figure out solutions. As each new obstacle is overcome, they become more certain that the vision can be reached.

Creating the vision comes before the design and the implementation. I know this seems obvious, but it needs to be said because some leaders get into these phases too quickly – before the vision is adequately formed. Any flaw in the vision will soon become apparent when the designers and implementers get started. By then, it can be too late and a leader can become a failure overnight.

Destiny implies that the vision will happen – regardless. Eventually, a human would get to the Moon. Once a leader develops a vision and they believe that it is destined to happen, they constantly ask themselves if they are the one who will lead.

Strong leaders believe in themselves. In some cases, it almost feels to them as if they had been chosen to lead. In reality, they are among a select group of humans who have the full range of leadership qualities and in a way 'nature' has selected/chosen them.

So let us take a look at some of the ways that a leader is inspired to create a vision of the future state.

Environment

I use the term 'environment' to mean everything that surrounds a person – people, circumstances and dynamics.

The rate at which the environment is changing has never been as rapid as it is now. That statement will be true forever, because the more sophisticated the human race becomes, the more it realizes that a change to a better place is needed. Mass communication has enabled the whole population to become aware of the need for change. It has even been suggested that change itself has been enabled through social networks. Visionary leaders read into the dynamics of the environment and see the need for change in a way that most of us miss. They interpret these dynamics in such a way that they form a vision of a future state which is a progression from the current state. The ability to 'join the dots' from 'here and now' to the future, a move which defines progress, is a key capability of a Visionary leader.

We can illustrate a model that inspires leaders to create a vision.

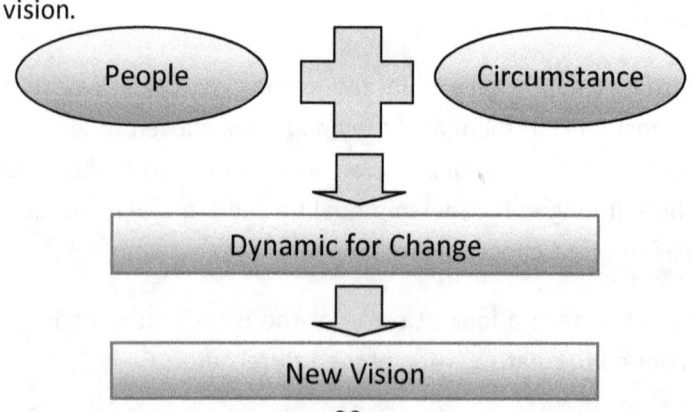

If people are living in an environment where there is oppression and poverty, then sooner or later a leader will emerge who will be brave enough to take on the forces in power and build a vision to liberate everyone; it is only a question of time. If people are living in an environment where they do repetitive work, then sooner or later a leader will emerge who will create a vision where machines do the work and humans are free to do more advanced tasks. These examples are commonplace in our history and illustrate how the environment influences leaders.

A leader who takes on the challenge of defining a better future must be brave. Bravery is a key characteristic of a leader and it is why some leaders eventually are regarded as heroes. Bravery compels a person to go into the 'unknown' – a place where no one has been. In many cases, everyone knows that a future state is possible, but few are brave enough to define it and gather support to start a journey to achieve it.

Circumstances and Events

The use of silicon in electronics was a key event in scientific development. This enabled the development of microprocessors which are at the core of all computers today. While this development was visible to everyone at the time, few had the vision to see how personal computing would significantly change the world.

Leaders anticipate and expect things to happen.

Major events are seen every day in the news and media. But leaders do not look exclusively to the media for their information. Events are reported <u>after</u> they happen. Leaders are more concerned about the circumstances that lead to an event <u>before</u> it happens.

In business, leaders engage heavily with their customers and the population at large and want to understand their difficulties and challenges. Business leaders are also close to developments and inventions coming out of research centres and universities. Leaders respond by creating a vision in which the future is a better place by making use of the information they have. So <u>anticipation</u> of a situation before it happens is a key characteristic of a leader. As an example, a business leader might anticipate that the general population will have increasing access to the Internet and begin to enable the company's products and services to be purchased online. Failing to anticipate this could let a competitor get ahead.

In government, leaders give a lot of thought to the future state of the country and try to create a vision that matches the desires of the population. Understanding the circumstances in which people live and anticipating the next event is key for a leader. A government that fails to respond to these circumstances will not survive. We need only look at many countries across the world where leaders failed to anticipate the level of disgruntlement of the population with the way their country was being run. Remember that many of those leaders were once heralded as heroes and liberators, but lost the ability to anticipate the way the population's own aspirations changed over time. It is even more remarkable that it was the population at large that had the new vision and not the country's leader.

Many events cannot be anticipated and a good leader can be measured by their reaction to such events.

9/11 is a key example.

An event like this was not foreseen by the U.S. administration. I recall that one of the key leaders to emerge in the aftermath of 9/11 was Rudy Giuliani – the Mayor of New York. His behaviours and comments were critical and earned him a great deal of respect. He was clear about his vision of restoring New York and was certain that an event of this type would never cause the ideals of the American people to falter.

Complacency can be fatal for a leader. Thinking that everything is fine in the current state and that there is no need for a future state is a disastrous position to adopt.

The Organization must Progress or it will Die.

And in order to progress, there must be a vision. And it is the primary function of the Visionary leader to define that vision.

Now I must inspire the rest of the organization

If a leader interprets events and circumstances and is inspired to create a vision, then the next step is to inspire others to follow. Failure to inspire others is a weakness that usually spells the end of the road for a leader. Sometimes the irony is that the vision is solid and does in fact represent a better place, but if a leader cannot garner support by inspiring others, the journey to the future state may never even start.

To inspire others requires some key characteristics in a leader. And the three dominant characteristics are *confidence, passion* and *self-belief*.

Leaders communicate their confidence, passion and self-belief by delivering speeches and through their writings. Over the past 100 years, technology has allowed us to see recordings of these and I am sure that many spring to mind. In all likelihood, some historical events would never have taken place unless the leader of the time inspired their followers through passionate speeches.

The ability to inspire others is one of the key attributes that sets a leader apart in society. And there is no educational programme I know of (formal or otherwise) that can teach a person to become inspirational.

I have often attended meetings where the majority of people have never met each other before and are asked to come up with the solution to some problem or devise some new process or service. If a leader emerges from within the group, I have always noticed that the key reason this happens is that someone inspires the group with a proposal. That's all it takes – the ability to inspire.

6.   I have a vision; tell me what's wrong with it?

So let's imagine that a leader has developed a vision for a future state. What now?

Most leaders should take time to reflect on the vision and go through a period of validation. Strong personal introspection and critique is essential before the vision is made public. It can be a great embarrassment for a leader to prematurely announce a vision and a graduate engineer point out a major flaw. Respect is gone, and for a leader respect is everything.

Strong leaders should always have at least two close colleagues that they can confide in. I call these people 'Validators' and the selection of the right people is critical for a Visionary leader:

1.   Always pick one validator who is <u>not</u> like you.

2.   Validators do not have to be part of the leadership team.

3.   Validators are not mentors.

Typically, Validators are rational people with a strong sense of pragmatism. They are usually <u>not</u> visionary by nature.

While they are positive and optimistic, they can be critical and find fault and weakness. They have very strong intuition and judgement, particularly about people. They provide the leader with insight to a whole range of vision validations. They take on the role of someone who would need to be convinced to buy into the vision and actively support it. They apply reason without ruling out the possibility of success. They do not jeer or ridicule an idea and they keep a confidence without question. No leader wants their unvalidated vision to leak through a trusted partner.

Equally, a Visionary leader needs a validator who can endorse their own pattern of thinking and may even add to the scope of the vision. Why put Facebook in universities and colleges alone when you can make it available to the world at large?

The leaders and the validators combine their strong intuition and judgement to form a conclusion. Either the vision is a better place and can be reached with appropriate design and implementation, or it is not. This is the point of no return for a Visionary leader.

Examples of successful vision would include the iPod and the communications satellite. An example of a failed vision would include the Sinclair C5 (go ahead and look it up). Not because the vision was questionable, but because the ability to build a reliable, safe, usable electric vehicle in 1985 was not something that could be designed and commercially implemented at that point in time.

And this brings me to a key aspect of vision.

Unless a vision has a strong chance of being achieved in a reasonable time, it will be regarded as a failure. The idea of a vehicle running for a long period on electricity (ideally sourced from renewable energy) is a common vision for early 21st century transportation leaders. This vision is right, but the validation is not. At least it hasn't been up to 2010 and certainly was not validated in 1985 when Sir Clive Sinclair tried.

So it is essential for the validation of a vision to ensure that when the leader begins to publicize the vision, and tries to influence others to support the vision, they will be successful.

There are some basic tests that a leader can apply to a vision:

1. Is the vision well defined and easy to understand?

2. Can it be achieved in a reasonable time?

3. Can it be achieved with reasonable and available resources and capabilities

The vision should be stated in one sentence and easily understood by everyone. I do not believe in hazy visions like "Let's build a machine that transports people from London to Sydney in 1 hour". Eh, no. Yes, the vision is the right one and one day it will happen. But this vision would fail a validation (today 2013) because it cannot be achieved in a reasonable time frame and there are no reasonable (i.e. commercially viable) technological resources available to achieve the vision. I would watch developments in engineering in the coming years and as soon as the engine that can achieve this vision is invented, then go into business.

Similarly, there was no point in trying to sell music over the Internet until the Internet had been developed with appropriate data transfer speeds.

In summary, try to avoid the "Let's solve world hunger" visions. Yes, the vision is noble and worthwhile, but not likely to happen with available resources, capabilities and commitment.

7.   Mission? Vision? What's the difference?

Most organizations have a vision and a mission.

The Vision is usually outlined as a highly aspirational goal. Typical examples would be "to be the best motor manufacturer in the world" or "to be the greatest research centre for cancer in the world."

A Mission, on the other hand, can be described in terms of achieving a significant step along the way towards reaching the vision.

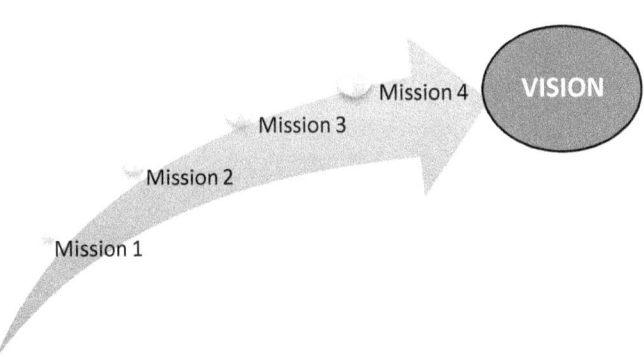

So if a football team has a vision to be the best in the world, the initial mission might be to win the domestic league before going on to another mission of winning the continental league.

Consider the vision of NASA in the 1960s to land man on the Moon and return them safely to Earth. In simplistic terms, we could look at this vision and an associated series of missions in the following way:

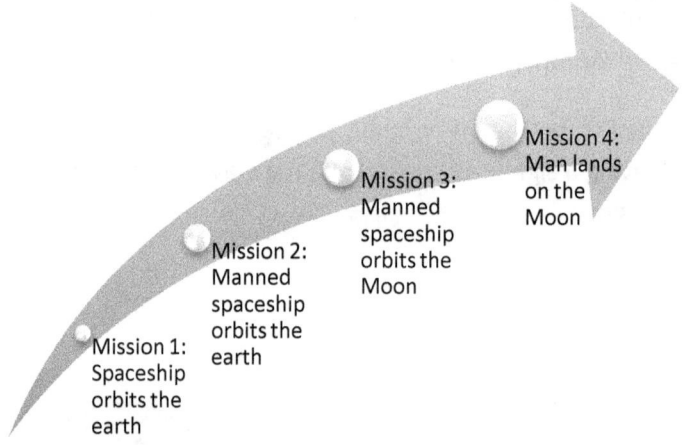

Mission 1: Spaceship orbits the earth

Mission 2: Manned spaceship orbits the earth

Mission 3: Manned spaceship orbits the Moon

Mission 4: Man lands on the Moon

When leaders put together visions for an organization, it is important to follow a small number of guidelines:

Let's get real

A vision must have a realistic chance of being achieved, but should be aspirational and stretch the capabilities and resources of the organization. The vision should outline goals that an organization can actually achieve. If a vision is beyond the point of aspirational, then it becomes a fictional wish. In such cases, there is a risk to morale in the organization as people feel that the vision is outside the boundaries of what they can achieve.

People in an organization should know and understand the vision of the organization and the current mission towards achieving that goal.

Take a random sample of 10 percent of any organization and ask them what the vision and mission is; chances are that the vast majority do not know.

Don't oversell

If an organization sets a vision to be the "best" or the "greatest", then there is a significant risk and this needs to be recognized.

A software company that sets its vision to be the best in the world may get very embarrassed if that same software is easily hacked and causes significant hardship to its users. Credibility of the vision and associated missions for the organization is essential and can be lost in a day.

Embarrassment hurts everyone in a company and no one feels comfortable when things go wrong. It is far better to achieve a modest vision than to fail in attempting an aspirational goal that is truly beyond the capability of the organization.

Nobody else can be as good as us – or can they?

If you set a vision to be "the one and only", "best of", you exclude the possibility that the rest of the human race is capable of being as good. Highly unlikely.

Many telecommunications companies around the world could not have imagined that a Scandinavian company could build innovative mobile phones and become one of the dominant names in the market. In turn, did anyone see a computer manufacturer becoming the dominant phone manufacturer in the early 21st century? In 1997 Apple's share price was just over $3. Fifteen years later it crossed the $500 mark. The US car industry probably didn't realise that Japanese cars would eventually become a dominant name in their market.

Basic human capability is evenly spread across the human race (there or thereabouts). Try to avoid any thoughts that you have a monopoly on capabilities.

Most organizations operate in a world where other organizations are trying to do something similar. In business, this is the basis of competition. When setting a goal for an organization, leaders must be realistic and understand the potential for other organizations to have the same (or a similar) goal.

Stay focused

Focus for everyone should be concentrated on a single point in time, with a clear and understandable description. Focus should allow everyone in the organization to see the part they play in contributing to the organization's ability to reach the current mission and ultimately achieve the vision.

Turning back to space exploration, the best story I ever heard about vision was this:

Back in the 1960s, a visitor to NASA is waiting patiently for a meeting to start and sees an older man working nearby. A conversation starts – probably about the weather. Finally, the visitor asks, "...and what do you do 'round here anyway?" Taking a sweeping brush to begin his shift, the man answers, "I put men on the moon."

The key point here is that every NASA employee knew the vision and <u>also</u> knew that whatever they did in the organization, they played a part in making it happen.

Here is NASA's vision:

> "NASA is charting a bold new course to the Cosmos, a journey that will take humans back to the Moon, and eventually to Mars and beyond."

I am quite sure that there are a number of missions on the way to achieving that vision:

- Participate in the building of the International Space Station.

- Develop a new launch vehicle beyond the shuttle.

- Put humans back on the Moon.

- Put humans on Mars

- ...and so on.

8. Building the Team

Visionary leaders create the vision.

Designers and Implementers get us there.

A critical phase for ensuring success is that the Design leader and Implementation leader fully understand the vision. To do this means we are going to have to get into a little bit more detail for these guys.

Designers are essentially strategists. They are organizational architects. They draw up high level plans. They make decisions about the nature of each mission. They are creative and innovative.

Implementers are builders. They work with resources (human and non-human). They work to a project time frame with a beginning, a middle and an end.

The key to success is that the Visionary leader, the Design leader and the Implementation leader work in total harmony. They have an outstanding level of communication, trust and understanding between them. No one person is at fault and no one person gets all the glory. They are equally passionate about achieving the vision. There are enormous levels of commitment and energy and nothing short of success is acceptable. Their energy permeates throughout the organization and eventually everyone shares their passion for achieving the goal.

A Design leader and an Implementation leader typically establish their own separate teams; often large teams. They must clearly articulate the vision and they are responsible for getting the organization to the destination. They have multiple choices and they must choose the right design and resources that will have the best chance of success. Some of the materials and resources may not exist and may need to be invented. Some of the expertise required is not available in the organization and will have to be acquired.

The outcome of what the designer decides is what we call the *Strategy*. Now the word 'strategy' is one of the most misused words in business. So let's be clear about what it means.

Vision describes "what" the future state looks like and implies the "when" and "where" it will happen (take a look at NASA's vision again).

Strategy describes "how" we get to the future state. A vision never describes how the journey will be made. That is the job of the designer and the implementer.

A lot of books have been written about strategy and I am not going to write another one here. The important thing is to understand in simple terms where strategy fits in when we talk about leadership.

In some ways, strategy is not the primary focus of Visionary leaders and it is often something they delegate. A Visionary leader is only concerned about achieving the goal in a reasonable time, with reasonable consumption of resources. How the journey is made is of importance to the Visionary leader because they want to have insight and approval of the strategy and be sure that whatever strategy is chosen, it will be the one that has the highest probability for success. But they may not be the one who develops the strategy.

From the outset I have said that an organization needs to have a single overall leader who assumes accountability for leading and managing the organization. It is usual for this person to be the Visionary leader (though not always) and I am going to assume that is the case for the purposes of illustration.

So an Organizational leader needs to establish a leadership team which, as I have said, needs to have design and implementation leadership capabilities. In a typical organization there are areas such as Finance, HR, Sales, Marketing and Production. However, this is a functional/management view of the organization and does not necessarily reflect the leadership capability.

The Organizational leader needs to clearly mark out the two senior teams in an organization and be clear about what is required to be a member of either/both teams. I can easily imagine a situation where the sales manager has clear organizational leadership skills and the finance manager does not. Being a member of the organizational leadership team requires a very different set of skills to those that are required by the functional/management team.

Managing this requires delicate interpersonal skills in order to keep everyone motivated as many senior managers will probably feel that they should be a part of the leadership team.

Let's start by taking a look at a typical functional/management team.

Functional/Management teams are primarily focused on sustaining the organization once the missions and visions have been achieved. Their goal is to build on the achievement and grow the organization organically until the next organizational vision/mission changes their instructions. For example, an organization develops and launches a new product. The management team will typically be responsible for ongoing Research & Development, manufacturing, marketing, sales, distribution and accounting.

Functional Management Team

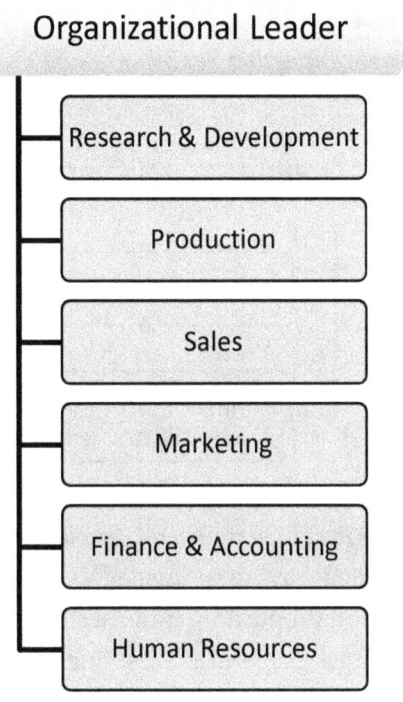

By contrast, an <u>Organizational Leadership</u> team should have four to six members and at its simplest level is made of the following:

<u>Organizational Leadership Team</u>

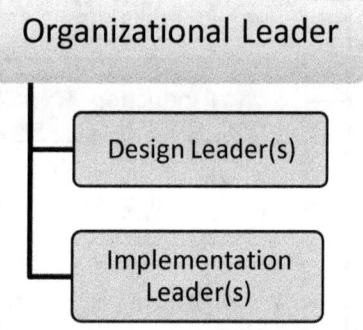

The roles of Design leader and Implementation leader should be filled by the managers of Research & Development and Production. If this were not the case, you would have to ask some searching questions about these individuals.

But these may not be the only leaders in the organization. For example, the sales manager or the HR manager might have significant leadership capabilities.

When bringing together a leadership team, it is critical to ensure that the correct quantity, quality and balance of leadership skills are present and it matters nothing whether they are all engineers or accountants as long as the ingredients are correct.

We can develop an organizational topography which outlines the key teams in an organization:

1. <u>Organizational Leadership Team</u>

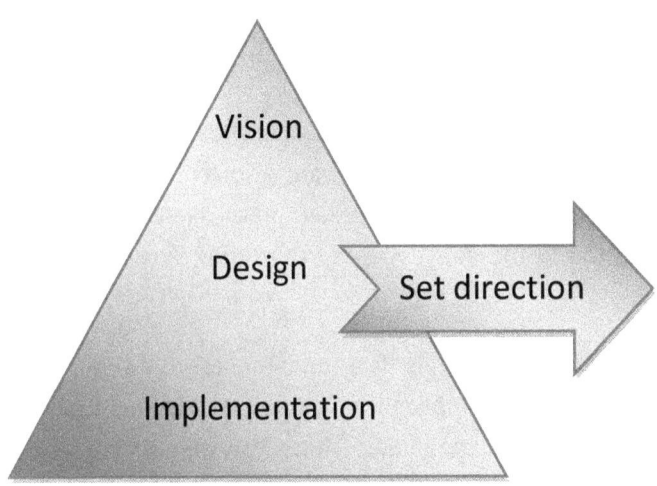

2. <u>Functional Management Team</u>

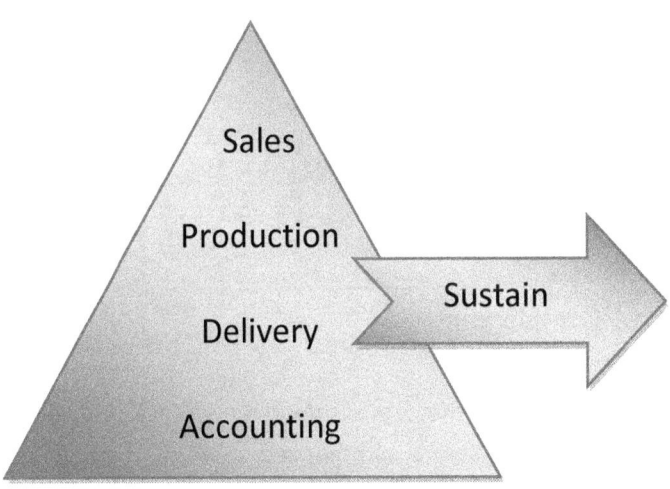

9. Have I got the right leadership team?

It is the responsibility of the Visionary leader to assess the leadership capability of the team and to hire and fire in order to ensure that the optimum team is in place. This is a hard job and the consequences of getting it wrong can be fatal.

Picking the 'right people' is a fundamental role of a leader. And this basically implies that the leadership team has the right leadership capabilities. These can be summarized as follows:

- **1. Aspiration and Vision**
- **2. Intuition and Judgement**
- **3. Influence**
- **4. Innovation**
- **5. Design**
- **6. Implementation**

Each individual on the team should be assessed against these capabilities and a summarized view of the overall team should be reviewed. The purpose of this review is to get a sense of the collective capabilities of the team and to understand the balance of capabilities.

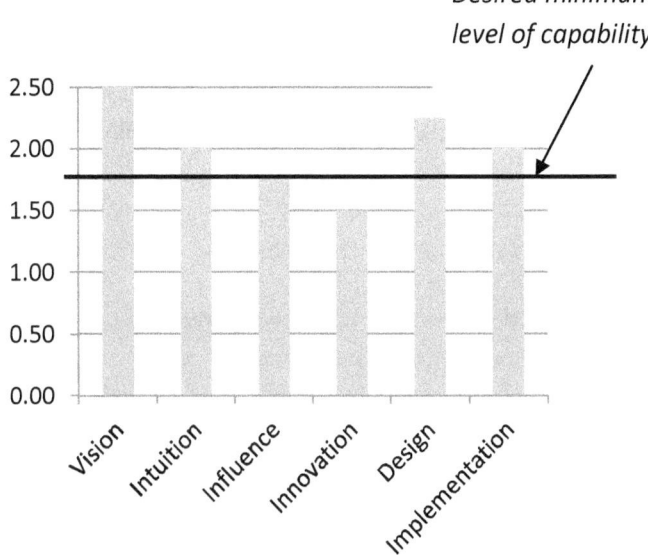

Desired minimum level of capability

This is not a truly scientific approach with a definite outcome, but will give indications of strengths and weaknesses.

To do this, you might consider using a scoring system as follows:

0 = no capability

1 = low capability

2 = standard capability

3 = high capability

In a perfect world, no one on the team should have a score of zero for any of the key skills. This would go against the principle that every leader in the team 'must have' at least a standard level of ability across the skills. In reality, people are part of a leadership team because they may have a very significant talent in one or more of the key skills. By contrast, they may be somewhat weak in other areas but the Organizational leader chooses to put them on the team primarily because of what they have and compensates elsewhere for their low-level capabilities.

Organizational leaders must evaluate the capability of the leadership team in the following terms:

1. There must be a significant capability for each skill.

2. Every member must be capable of making notable contributions.

In addition, there are some 'rules of thumb' for assessing the competence of the leadership. This should be applied in conjunction with your own intuition about the individuals on the team. Make suitable allowances for those who have the potential to develop and improve their contributions by being part of a leadership team:

1. There should be a least one '3' for every capability.

2. Carefully review any person who has more than one 'zero'.

3. Typical average for each capability should 1.75 to 2.00.

4. Typical average for each person should be 1.75 (review participants with a score below this).

Let's take a few examples in which we look at a six-person leadership team (including the Organizational leader). In these examples, and purely for the purposes of illustration, I am including a sales manager, as well as a finance and HR manager who have all been determined to have some organizational leadership skills.

a) <u>Overall, a balanced team</u>

	Vision	Intuition	Influence	Innovation	Design	Implement	Total	Average
Visionary Leader	3	3	2	1	2	2	13	2.2
Head of R&D	1	2	1	3	3	2	12	2.0
Production Manager	2	3	0	1	1	3	10	1.7
Sales Manager	0	1	1	3	2	2	9	1.5
Finance	3	1	3	0	0	2	9	1.5
HR	2	3	3	1	2	2	13	2.2
Total	11	13	10	9	10	13	66	
Average	1.8	2.2	1.7	1.5	1.7	2.2		

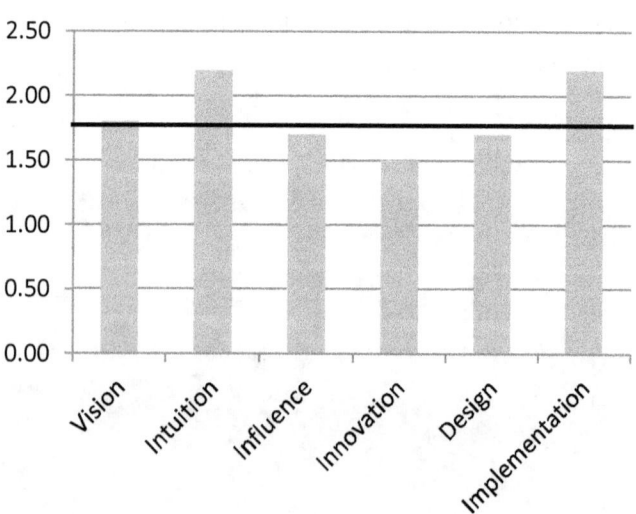

- A strong team with at least one '3' held by every person and one '3' in every capability.

- There is a question about the participation of the finance manager in the leadership as he/she has two zeros.

- Need to be careful that the Visionary leader and the finance leader do not get too engaged in debate about the vision.

- Very strong intuition is a key asset.

- Visionary leader needs to utilize the influential capability of the finance and HR leader.

- Design is reliant on one person and they will be critical to success.

- Sales manager lacks skills around vision, intuition and influence and is purely a 'get things done' person. Perhaps they are a new or younger addition to the team who is very pragmatic. Watch for conflict with the visionary types as this person can often put obstacles in the way.

b) Great vision, but we will ever get there?

	Vision	Intuition	Influence	Innovation	Design	Implement	Total	Average
Visionary Leader	3	3	2	1	1	1	11	1.8
Head of R&D	2	1	1	1	3	1	9	1.5
Production Manager	2	0	0	2	1	3	8	1.3
Sales Manager	1	2	0	1	1	2	7	1.2
Finance	3	0	1	1	0	0	5	0.8
HR	2	2	1	0	0	1	6	1.0
Total	13	8	5	6	6	8	46	
Average	2.2	1.3	0.8	1.0	1.0	1.3		

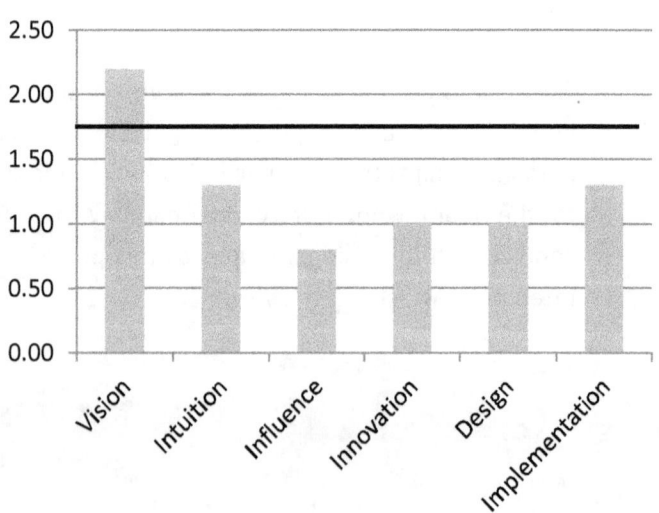

- A team with a very strong capability to develop a vision. Likely to lead to some conflict as there is no guarantee that everyone will have the same vision.

- Significant imbalances across some of the capabilities and obvious weaknesses in influence, innovation and design.

- Lack of influence will cause this team to struggle to get sponsorship.

- Lack of innovation may mean that great visions may never get implemented.

- Three capabilities have a score of 1.0 or less and this represents a weakness.

- One member of the team (finance) has a very low average score of 0.8 and may not be a significant contributor.

c) Individual Visionary?

	Vision	Intuition	Influence	Innovation	Design	Implement	Total	Average
Visionary Leader	3	0	0	1	2	1	7	1.2
Head of R&D	2	1	2	2	3	2	12	2.0
Production Manager	1	1	1	2	2	3	10	1.7
Sales Manager	0	1	2	3	1	2	9	1.5
Finance	2	1	2	1	0	0	6	1.0
HR	2	1	3	1	1	1	9	1.5
Total	10	5	10	10	9	9	53	
Average	1.7	0.8	1.7	1.7	1.5	1.5		

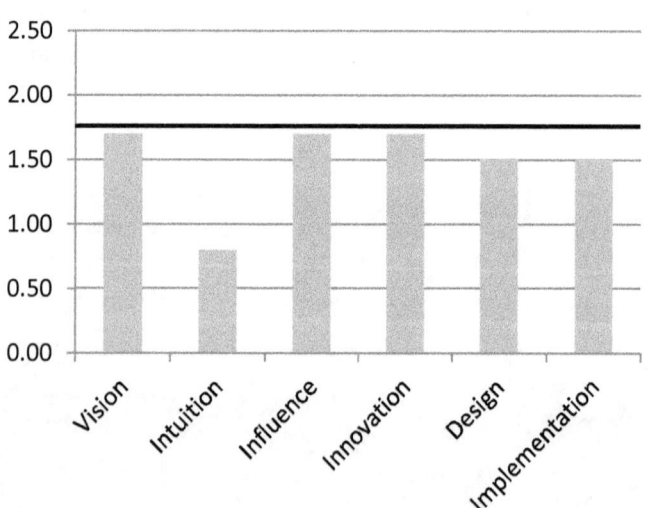

Analysis:

- The Visionary leader is missing some key leadership skills (intuition and influence) and this can happen in a situation where a visionary <u>individual</u> with a 'clever idea' is trying to assemble a team to make it a reality.

- No other leader is strong in 'intuition' to compensate for the Visionary leader and this is likely to result in poor judgment around key aspects such as finance, resourcing, marketing, etc.

- The head of R&D is likely to have conflict with the Visionary leader in a battle of pragmatism versus aspiration.

- Visionary leader should consider adding another person to the team.

This is a simple approach to assessing a leadership team and is certainly worth doing as an exercise. If you try it, get an objective view from someone outside the group.

10. Individual Visionary

When an organization is first created, it is usually started by an *Entrepreneurial Visionary*. This person may have invented or innovated and have a vision to develop a new product or service. They may have a vision for the future state of society. Whatever the vision is, we need to understand that they may not be equipped with all the skills necessary to lead the organization.

Individual visionaries are not automatically equipped with leadership and organizational skills. Inventers and innovators who attempt to take on the leadership role are taking a gamble. The gamble is that, in addition to their highly developed visionary and innovative skills, they are adequately equipped with other leadership skills including influence and intuition.

An individual visionary usually has high vision, innovation and design skills. They often lack the judgment and influence necessary to make the vision a reality. This can be a significant impediment to success. They often feel that they need to play a central role in every activity. They put themselves in the spotlight at every possible occasion, only to lack the ability to influence key sponsors and supporters. They can often lack personal 'presence' and come across as uncomfortable when they step outside the Research &

Development environment and into the business environment

Of course this is not always true. Bill Gates had vision, innovation, intuition and influence skills when he first convinced IBM to buy the DOS operating system for their first personal computer. But how many Bill Gates are there?

I am convinced that many great ideas are sitting on shelves around the world because the visionary individuals lack organizational design and implementation skills. When this happens, a visionary individual should acquire the design and implementation capability. In the commercial world, these can be venture capital (VC) companies or independent investors.

It is true that VCs put money into fledgling ideas in order to make them a reality; after all, this is one way that an inventor/innovator gets their idea off the ground and how a VC company makes money. However, a VC puts in resources other than money and these are typically the leadership and management skills that are not always present in the beginning.

Any visionary individual who does not have the resources to make their vision a reality is often forced to sell a portion of the business in return for finance. But it is equally important to get the leadership skills that come with the money.

The important thing for a visionary individual to do is get a full and thorough personality profile of themselves. This will help point out their strengths and capabilities as well the skills that they may be missing.

11. *Something tells me this is wrong*

Intuition is a vital leadership skill and is the <u>sole</u> difference between success and failure. Intuition is used all the time and in every situation to <u>make decisions</u>.

Leaders make a lot of decisions. Where to go, what to do, when to do it, how to do it, why to do it a particular way.

And everyone is watching.

As soon as you make your first bad decision, you are in recovery mode. Make a second and it could be fatal. Make a third and it is almost certainly fatal.

If you are not making decisions, then you are not leading. Ask yourself how many decisions passed before you today.

Leaders have different approaches to making decisions. Some people can take in all the data, turn it into information, apply some wisdom and, hey presto, they have a decision. All in a few moments. Some people are reflective. They take time to consider. They talk it over with close associates and advisors and after a few days they announce their decision.

There is no formula for making decisions in order to get the right answer every time. There are, however, some guidelines.

Gather the facts

Many leaders gather a lot of data. Average consumption of electricity per household, time spent travelling to work every day. These are data points describing particular activities or events – all of which have occurred in the past.

A leader utilizes a considerable wealth of resources to get data and in the world of the Internet and online databases this has become quite easy.

Turn data into information

A leader must summarize what the data is 'saying' by turning it into information. And information is key to making a decision.

Try to remember that almost everyone can get access to data and 'common' information. But only intuitive leaders turn data into <u>insightful</u> information. To have sole possession of insightful information puts an organization in a position of considerable strength. This is difficult in today's world, where data and information are pervasive. The omission of data can result in an incomplete information set and a leader needs to be careful to ensure they are looking at the matter from every angle.

Taking time to decide

There is no hard guideline about how long a leader should take to make a decision. But remember that a leader will be under very close observation as the rest of the team/organization waits patiently to hear the decision. Leaders who appear to ponder decisions can be easily labelled as indecisive and lacking leadership. Leaders who appear to make decisions too quickly can easily be regarded as impetuous and lacking all the necessary information.

Making wise decisions

When a leader has all the information laid out in front of them, they must make a decision.

There are only three outcomes:

1. Okay, let's do it.

2. No. I don't think this is right.

3. I need more information.

The third option simply results in the collection of more data and a new information set.

Saying 'Yes' or 'No' is the only real outcome.

Leaders use their wisdom to make a decision and wisdom comes from a number of things:

1. The feeling of just plain 'common sense'.

2. The feeling that the way to go is 'obvious'.

3. Extrapolation. The knowledge and/or experience of something similar having occurred in the past that resulted in a particular outcome. Since nothing can ever be repeated in exactly the same way as before, a leader must make the necessary adjustments to arrive at a conclusion.

4. The balance of risk versus certainty. History will likely repeat itself if you repeat everything as it was done in the past. But if a leader is embarking on a road to a future state that is better than the current state, it is logical that the future state is not like any previous or current state. Therefore history will not repeat itself. As a result there will always be an element of risk and the leader must balance the level of risk taken against the certainty of the outcome.

5. Insight. Bringing together past experience, knowledge, data, information and an evaluation of all future outcomes. This can often be referred to as the 'voice inside you' telling you that something is right or wrong.

6. Enlightenment. A very strong feeling that a particular outcome can and will happen.

- Common Sense
- It's obvious
- Extrapolation
- Insight
- Enlightenment

This view of intuition may seem overly complicated but it is important to understand that a leader will use this skill more than any other to answer key questions:

What vision represents progress?

Who should I choose for my team?

How will I influence sponsors?

What design has the best chances of success?

12. What Designers have

Designers are complex individuals. They see the end game and they see the multitude of paths that can ensure the goal is achieved. Now I am not suggesting that they work like the GPS in your car and figure out all the possible paths between A and B and simply choose the shortest, most efficient route.

No. That's not how designers work.

They are intuitive and have a strong ability to use their judgement in determining the best option. They leverage their experiences wisely. They are positive and balanced about what is achievable. They move the boundaries of what is achievable today and create a new boundary for what can be achieved tomorrow.

Designers are innovative with the resources they have at their disposal. They may even combine resources together to create a new resource. And, finally, they may have to invent some new technologies and processes of their own.

In the context of leadership and organizational progress, designers should not be regarded as designers of aesthetically beautiful items such as clothes, jewellery, cars, buildings, and so on. These are artists – not designers.

Designers are strategists. They figure out the <u>optimal route</u> which allows an organization to reach the future state. They plan the scope for each mission that will be achieved along the journey. And they achieve this in the following way:

1. Apply innovation at all times

Optimize the use of resources and capabilities

2. Design a route that is achieveable in a reasonable time

Establish the path of least resistance and optimum efficiency

3. Ensure sustainability when we get there

Conserve resources and capabilities in order to survive

<u>Being innovative with resources and capabilities</u>

Innovation is at the core of every organization's survival and achievements. Innovation means that you apply new processes and technologies to create a new product or service. Airplanes today are very different to airplanes of 50 years ago. And if you make airplanes, you should be thinking about how they will be different in 10 years' time. If you don't, someone else will.

Innovation can also mean combining other innovations and inventions to create a new product. For example, the invention of the flat-screen display was key to the development of laptop computers.

In general, leaders are focused on two types of innovation:

1. *Product/Service Innovation*

2. *Strategic Innovation*

Product and Service innovation is concerned with what the organization produces and strategic innovation is concerned with how an organization develops and survives.

In the context of organizational development, Design leaders are focused on strategic innovation. This involves the creative use of resources and capabilities to bring an organization forward.

Design leaders have three ways to utilize resources and capabilities:

1. Utilize the existing resources and capabilities of people and equipment within the organization.

2. Invest in upskilling and upgrading existing resources and capabilities.

3. Acquire expertise from the outside.

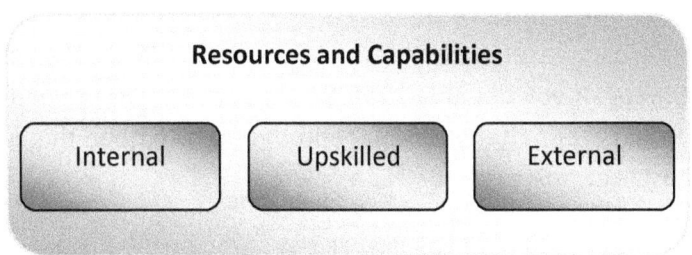

Resources and Capabilities

Internal   Upskilled   External

Most organizations use all three types of resources and capabilities. Many car manufacturers do not build their own engines but choose to acquire engines from other car companies. This allows an organization to focus on its own core capability. If your key area of capability is to design highly functional mobile phones, then why spend time trying to figure out how to build the battery?

Organizations develop close partnerships with technology companies in order to utilize new and advanced equipment. Industrial robots have allowed manufacturers to improve on the time required to build a product, improve quality and reduce costs.

Organizations constantly invest in upskilling their people and this is an essential investment in the future capability of an organization. Any organization that does not have a significant budget for training and development is not likely to grow.

Finding the right balance and combination of internal capabilities, upskilled capabilities and external capabilities is a key skill of the Design leader in developing a strategy.

Getting there in a reasonable time

Time can be an ally or an enemy when developing a strategy. If you design a strategy to achieve the vision and you get there after your competitor gets there, then this is most likely to be regarded as a failure.

The race to put a human in space was won by the Russians. Although the U.S. had a good design and achieved their vision, the timing was wrong. So the successful achievement of the vision is remembered in history as coming second.

But we should always remember that the primary goal is to achieve the future state and the secondary goal is to do so before someone else. The U.S. were still able to build on the success of putting a man in space, which ultimately led to them putting a man on the Moon.

Ensuring sustainability

The strategy to achieve the organization's vision cannot consume all the resources. If you reach the future state and have no capability to build on what you have achieved, then the future state will die and the organization will regress.

The cost of reaching the future state must be recovered by what is achieved. Let's suppose you have a vision to build a car that uses very low amounts of fossil fuel. But if that car costs four times the price of a conventional car, then the cost of achieving the goal may be too high. A strategy must be developed whereby the cost of getting there does not outweigh the cost of staying there.

In reality, sustaining a future state must be regarded as a short-term objective as an organization will need a new vision to progress further.

A strategy can be copied once it is revealed. Achieving a vision at the second attempt can often mean that it is achieved more efficiently. If you have utilized capabilities outside your organization, there is nothing to stop others doing the same. Sustainability only comes from your core capability, which you can protect.

A soccer club that develops a strategy to bring in young talented players and develop them over a three-year period would seem to make sense. But this design can be copied. What cannot be copied is the core capability to evaluate young players and determine which of them have the ability to be the best players in the future.

In the modern era, companies are spending more and more money protecting their achievements. This is typically done by filing patents and registered trademarks. Protecting the achievement is a key part of any strategy.

13. What Implementers have

Implementers are the first to reach the destiny. If the vision is to build a new product, they are the first to see it working.

Implementers have perseverance. They believe in the future state as outlined by the vision. They are motivated by the glory of getting to the future state.

Implementers face obstacles every day and are creative in overcoming them. What is particularly significant about these obstacles is that many of them <u>cannot be anticipated in advance</u>. Regardless, they act quickly and efficiently with their resources, remain positive, and get around the challenge in order to move forward.

Implementers are innovative and work closely with Design leaders to figure out the optimum way to utilize resources and capabilities. Implementers are also concerned with the effectiveness and efficiency of *processes and plans* that will be used to bring the organization forward.

Design leaders will have outlined the strategy. But we must not forget that a strategy is nothing more than a theory. A concept. A possibility. A probability. A likelihood. Only through the skills of an Implementation leader will it become a reality.

Implementers are practitioners. They get things done. There is a real and tangible outcome to their work.

Implementation leaders <u>love</u> success. In the extreme, they love it more than their own lives. The famous explorer David Livingstone was once travelling in a part of Africa which was said to be inhabited by a tribe known for their dislike of the 'white man' and their practice of cannibalism. Fear of failure was greater than the fear he had of losing his life and he continued his journey despite the risks.

Implementation leaders are heroes. They achieve the goal despite the difficulties that they face. They walk a path that no other human has walked and ultimately achieve great success for the organization.

If you are a Visionary leader, make sure you pick the best Implementation leader that you can get. It all depends on them.

Implementers have a repertoire of key skills necessary to bring the organization to the future state:

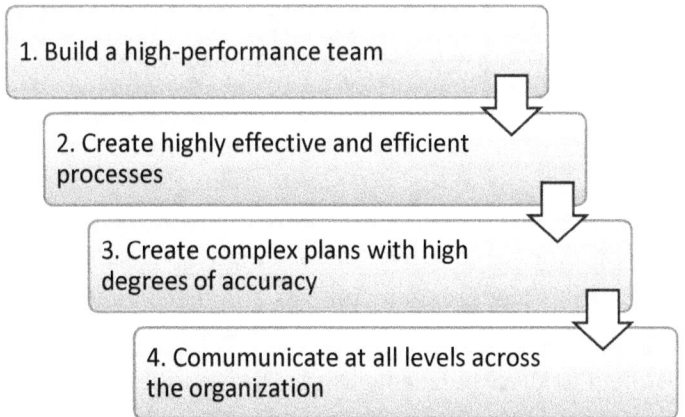

1. Build a high-performance team

2. Create highly effective and efficient processes

3. Create complex plans with high degrees of accuracy

4. Comumunicate at all levels across the organization

Building high-performance teams

Implementers rarely work alone. They assemble a team. They allocate the players on the team to specific tasks. These people may, in turn, assemble other teams. What is essential here is the ability to *pick the right people for the job that maximizes each person's capability*. This can be the most critical skill of an Implementation leader. The entire success of reaching the goal often rests on carefully selecting and utilizing the right people. So much is at stake that an Implementation leader will think nothing of offloading a resource that fails to live up to their expectation. So expect a certain amount of impatience.

In contrast, Implementers are highly motivational people. They inspire the team. They have confidence and passion and express it emotionally. They constantly seek out ways to get the highest performance from the team.

Create highly effective and efficient processes

Design leaders will have figured out the strategy for utilizing internal and external resources and capabilities as well as deciding what investment to make in new resources and capabilities. Implementation leaders work very closely with Design leaders in this task.

It is equally important to choose the most effective and efficient process to apply to resources and capabilities. Choosing an inappropriate process for the organization's resources and capabilities can significantly impact the roadmap to success. Quality can be impacted if a process is deficient. Costs can be increased if a process is over-engineered or excessively bureaucratic.

Design leaders are usually people with outstanding abilities in process and have extensive knowledge of the latest methodologies.

Communication

The relationship between the Visionary leader and the Implementation leader is key. Implementers are empowered to do everything they can to make the vision a reality. Implementers are expected to keep the Visionary leader updated on progress. When an obstacle is reached there will always be the temptation to obscure the difficulty and keep the Visionary leader out of the loop. If the implementer reports the difficulty it must be done in a way to ensure that everyone feels the problem can be overcome.

So communication is a key skill required by an Implementation leader. They must be capable of communicating at all levels across the organization.

Being a highly skilled planner

Implementers typically work to a plan. This is the first time that the leadership team can see a tangible roadmap that takes an organization to its vision.

Let us consider the example of an airline that has a vision to become a 'total travel business', incorporating hotel, car rental and tours into their total product offering. The designers develop a strategy to utilize the Internet to sell the product and form alliances with third party companies to provide the hotels, cars and tours. The implementers map out a plan which shows who the partners are, how and when the systems will be built and the total cost in terms of resources and capabilities. This is the <u>first test</u> that the vision is achievable. Passing the test gives inspiration and motivation to all.

As the implementation progresses, implementers update and modify the plan continually. This occurs because of one or more of the following:

- The strategy (theory) does not play out as expected – most likely because some of the assumptions fail to happen.

- Unforeseen obstacles get in the way and a change to the design or roadmap is required.

- Resources get consumed at unexpected rates.

- The capabilities are below the level required to be successful.

The Implementation leader responds to these challenges by doing one of the following:

1. First and foremost, modify the implementation plan and still achieve the goal.

2. Suggest a change to the design which will still allow the vision to be achieved. This also requires a change to the implementation plan.

3. Suggest a change to the vision which will still allow the organization to achieve a future state that represents progress. This also requires a change to the design and the implementation plan.

Implementation leaders do not like failure. If they fail to reach the future state then the investment in the new vision will not be realized. It is bad enough that the organization does not progress, but it is most likely to be the Implementation leader who delivers the 'bad news' to the leadership team. In addition, the Implementation leader may be held responsible (often unfairly) for not bringing the organization forward.

14. Invention and Innovation

Innovation and creativity play a central role in helping an organization reach its goals. And when the goal is reached, an organization must protect its position and build value.

To begin, let's take a moment to understand Invention and Innovation.

New and unique

Invention is the development of a new device or process. The key part of an invention is that it is 'new'. Nobody has ever seen it before and that implies that it is unique.

The human race has been in the 'inventing' business for a long time (was the wheel the first invention?). Notable phases include the invention of mechanical devices. For example, the invention of the weaving machine was a significant step forward in the mass production of clothes. When electronics came along, inventions moved to electro-mechanical devices and the progression has continued to the world of integrated circuits and software.

Equally, a process or methodical approach can be characterized as an invention.

An invention in and of itself can sometimes be of no real value to anyone and therefore we should not assume that an invention has a commercial value. Many inventions sit on shelves or in patent offices waiting to be utilized. It may be 'ahead of its time' in the context that no one has figured out what to use it for. However, most are of value and make life easier for everyone.

Consider some common inventions:

- The altimeter. Of no practical use in and of itself, but tremendously valuable in an airplane.

- The battery. Again, only valuable as long as there is something useful to provide energy to (such as a bulb).

- The Biro pen

- The laser

- The light bulb

- Paper

- The telephone

Combination and commercial value

Innovations are quite a different thing.

I will put forward the meaning of innovation to be the combination of one or more existing inventions and innovations to create something new that has practical use and is likely to have commercial value. The emphasis here is that it is 'new', that it is a 'combination' and also that it has 'commercial value'.

Perhaps the classic example of innovation is the Internet. This combines a number of inventions (computers, telecommunications, processes, protocols, and so on) to create a mass communication system. What is important here is that a computer is used in combination with telecommunications devices in a unique way to create something new.

The computer itself is an innovation as it brought together micro-electronics, television monitors, keyboards and software. The TV monitor was invented for a long time before the computer was invented. Similarly, the keyboard was invented and used in typewriters. And programmable integrated circuits had been around for a while. It is the unique combination of these items, along the accompanying software, that was innovative.

The blur between the two

Yes. It can often be difficult to truly determine if something is an invention or an innovation. But let's not get too pedantic here. For the purposes of leadership let's differentiate between the two by saying that both are 'new' and can be a device or a process. An innovation can 'combine' inventions and innovations and is focused on creating something that has 'commercial value'.

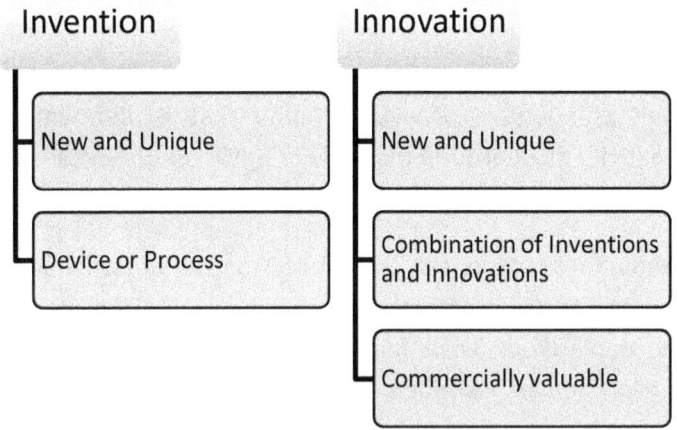

Invention	Innovation
New and Unique	New and Unique
Device or Process	Combination of Inventions and Innovations
	Commercially valuable

Being creative

An organization must be creative in order to survive. In this context, being 'creative' means that a person or organization has the ability to invent and/or innovate.

Creativity can function at two levels in an organization:

1. The Product/Service Level

2. The Operational Level

Product creativity

Every organization provides a product or a service. This is true for commercial organizations as well as the local 'keep your town tidy' organization.

As creativity is the only way to build products and services, it stands to reason that an organization must possess this capability. Leaders must be able to evaluate and quantify the creative ability of their organization as well as that of their competitors. An organization that is deficient in creativity must acquire it quickly or it will risk the possibility of regression.

Product innovators can be pioneers or imitators. Pioneers aim to create something entirely new (Sony Walkman or the Apple iPod), while imitators look to create something similar to an existing product but apply operational innovation (see below) to make it cheaper, more reliable, etc.

Operational creativity

An organization can apply creativity to the day-to-day way in which it operates and this can create as much of an advantage as the product that it delivers.

Regardless of whether an organization acts as a pioneer or an imitator in the product they deliver, they can still apply operational innovation. Operational innovation focuses on creating a culture of creativity in which everyone is expected to come up with ideas for improvement. The person who works in the customer support centre could easily make suggested improvements to the product based on the customer feedback they hear. Only in an organization that promotes creativity will this person feel free to express their thoughts.

In some cases an organization can tend to focus too much on the product and not enough on the operation. There are many outcomes to this. For example, we have seen prestigious car brands severely damaged because although the car was quite advanced, it was unreliable because of poor operational processes which lacked quality.

Here are some examples of operational creativity:

- Efficient manufacturing processes that have a low number of defects, thereby reducing cost and improving quality (6 Sigma).

- Processes that allow customers to purchase a product to their own specifications (Dell computers).

- Highly efficient stock management (Amazon).

- Application of lean manufacturing to eliminate waste and duplication.

- Application of the Internet to allow customers place orders online.

- Deciding on the right mix of 'build our own' and/or 'buy from others'.

Imitators tend to apply operational innovation to create something that is cheaper, faster, more reliable, is custom built, has slightly more features, and so on. It is this operational innovation that once gave companies like Dell the advantage over IBM.

As a leader, what should I focus on?

Visionary leaders paint a picture of a future state and this is almost entirely related to the product/service provided by the organization. The vision may be to create a new product, or to enhance an existing one, or to sell more products in other markets. Whatever it is, it typically relates to the product.

Design and Implementation leaders tend to focus on operational creativity. They are primarily focused on the utilization of available resources to reach the goal and creativity is an essential skill in this area.

What is important is that a leader must be creative. This is a 'must have'. Equally, it is important to recognize that every organization will possess creativity in varying degrees across the leadership team. Therefore, the Organizational leader must be willing to acquire creative skills when necessary and replenish them if they leave.

15. Why I need to influence people

There are very few situations where a leader can go it alone. That is, where a leader can create the vision, design the path and implement the roadmap – all on their own.

Leaders need others. But most of all, leaders need to influence others. The key to influencing people is to understand what motivates them. Everyone is free to join whatever organization they wish. So leaders must attract and retain the talent they need to ensure the organization is successful. Influencing talented people is a key requirement of every leader.

Equally, leaders may not have all the resources they need to meet the goals outlined in the vision. So leaders must use their influencing skills to attract external support. This can be in the form of a financial contribution or investment, but can also be an endorsement.

You yourself

It is important for every leader to appreciate that influencing people comes primarily from you yourself. No one can step in and do this for you. You must do it yourself. Your character and personality are key components in how you project an image of yourself and people either like it or they don't. Remember this – it is important. People will either like you or they won't.

How you communicate the vision has the ability to excite people to join in or it can turn them off and they will opt out. A leader must adapt their style of communication to suit their audience and this is key in the influencing process. Equally important is self-belief and trust. If people believe that a leader can take the organization forward and that they can be trusted, they will be influenced to follow them.

So let's take a look at the various ways in which leaders look to influence people:

1. There is something in it for you.

2. There is something in it for the organization.

3. There is something in it for the wider community or country.

So what is the 'something'?

People are motivated by two things:

1) Financial reward

2) Achievement

Financial reward allows people to take care of the basic human needs such as food, clothing, somewhere to live, the ability to look after the family, further education, and so on.

Achievement allows people to feel a greater sense of worth in the wider community. This is a key component to human nature. People who have accumulated large sums of money through successful business ventures are primarily driven because of their inner need for further achievement. There comes a point where the money does not matter.

There is something in it for everyone

First and foremost a leader must influence the individual. Leaders must understand what motivates an individual. I have discussed the basic human needs which can be taken care of by financial reward. But let's not forget that financial reward will also be necessary to ensure that an individual achieves some or all of their personal life goals. An individual may want to travel the world, contribute to a charity that they feel a strong affinity towards, create a legacy, and so on. All of these require money.

Leaders influence people by holding out the possibility of financial reward which is dependent on the achievement of the vision. This 'carrot' approach is very common in modern business. Leaders should be cautious in the over-application of financial reward as it can have a negative impact by inducing inappropriate behaviour among the key people in the organization. Examples of this behaviour include covering up mistakes, apportioning blame to others, making others look like poor performers, and so on. Ultimately the risk is that people perform as individuals and not as a team. Leaders should consider financial reward which is based on an individual's performance as well as the performance of the organization as a whole.

Once the financial reward has been established it is equally important for a leader to establish a sense of accomplishment that will come as a result of the organization achieving its goal through the vision.

In a commercial organization, one key influencer will be the possibility of promotion once the goal is achieved. If not promotion, then a significant step on the path towards promotion.

Many organizations are focused on motivating and influencing their employees by aligning the vision with an external cause which is good for the wider community. Oil companies produce oil and when the oil is utilized, it creates pollution. But some oil companies are aligning themselves with 'Green Energy', which is good for the environment and produces less pollution. This form of 'parallel' vision for an organization has a positive motivational impact and influence on individuals.

In non-commercial organizations such as charities, sport, exploration and human rights, achievement is the key inspirational motive which influences people. It can be so strong that some people will forego financial reward just to be part of the organizational achievement.

Some people can be motivated to achieve a goal for the wider organization, community or even their country. Again, financial reward plays a small part in the influencing process here. Being part of a community project, representing your local county at a national event, playing sport for your country are all strong motivators and the prospect of achievement at this level can be a very strong influence on individuals.

Leaders must be able to create the appropriate reward to influence the person to play a part in the organization's journey towards its vision.

Influencing outsiders who are enablers

Most organizations need the input of external players in order to achieve the vision. So while leaders must try to influence people to participate at first hand in the organization itself, it is equally important for a leader to influence external players to contribute. External players can provide key resources and capabilities:

- Financial investment

- Expertise

- Endorsement

The challenge facing leaders is that external players are in constant demand for their contribution and a leader will need to compete with others just to get an audience. Have you ever had a really good business idea? Have you ever tried to get 30 minutes with a potential investor? Having got the 30 minutes and made the pitch, have you influenced them sufficiently to invest? Try it. It's not easy.

Looking for an endorsement is just as hard if not harder than influencing people to give you money. Endorsement means that someone agrees with the purpose of your vision. This becomes a public statement which speaks to their reputation. An endorser will need to have a great deal of trust in you because you could significantly embarrass them if you fail. If you fail in achieving the goal, it may never be seen in the media. If you embarrass an endorser who is famous, it will definitely hit the headlines.

Using a network to influence people

Leaders do not know everyone, so how do you influence someone who knows nothing about you or your vision? The key here is to influence someone you <u>do</u> know who, in turn, can influence the person you need. And to do this, you need to have a network of people who know you. This is why so many business leaders put a lot of effort into building a network of people outside their organization.

The goal of the network is to establish a relationship with other people. This relationship must be built on trust. Perhaps you have worked together on a project or in a company. Perhaps you have done business with the person in the past. Whatever the basis for getting to know other people and expand your network, it is an essential tool in influencing people who do not know you.

Using a network can set you on the fast track to getting the help you need. If you know someone who works with a venture capital company, I would say that you would get an audience to make your business pitch quite quickly.

Persistence

Okay, so you are just out of college, you do not know anyone of importance and influence and you want to get the attention of a potential investor.

The only way is through persistence. Call, write, phone, send flowers. Send flowers to someone who knows them. Persevere. Everyone admires people who try hard and eventually you will get your moment.

Never give up.

Try to persevere beyond the point at which you become a nuisance. And you will eventually become a nuisance.

The risk with this approach is that when you do get your moment, your audience will probably only listen to you in order to hear you out and not because they're interested in your proposal. Therefore, your delivery must be outstanding. In this situation, you can only influence someone through your character and personality.

Events can influence

People can be influenced by events. A famine in Africa heavily influenced a group of pop/rock stars to raise money to help those affected. Their vision was to run a music event on a global scale to raise funds. They also exerted tremendous influence over politicians by generating popular mass support for changes in the way the developed world supported the poorer nations and peoples of Africa.

A leader's response to an event has the ability to exert influence over a large number of people – quickly.

When key events happen, make sure that you are in front of your organization and external enablers as soon as possible. Communicate your feelings and thoughts. Speak truthfully. If your vision is not impacted, say so. If the vision is impacted, say so. Do not project uncertainty. If you are not in a position to give a perspective on the event, promise to come back and give a further update – soon.

Key events can have a positive or negative effect on the vision of the organization. But a leader can use an event to influence people in a dramatic way and how effective the influence will be is down to the leader's behaviour.

Coercion

Coercion is the use of force to influence people to behave in a particular way. You might think this is a dangerous course of action for any leader to take. But believe me, coercion is used by leaders much more than you would think.

Consider the situation where a leader wants to bring a key expert into the team to work on a new vision for the organization. Let us imagine that the expert is happy to stay where they are in the company and are not keen to make the change. Perhaps the expert does not believe that the vision can be achieved. A leader who feels that the expert is critical to their success may use their position of authority to coerce the expert to join up. Leaders can suggest that by not joining the project, the expert could suffer a reversal to their career progression or to their annual bonus. A leader may even go as far as saying that if the expert refuses to join the project, they should not expect to get any support if they find themselves in 'difficult circumstances' at a latter point.

This may feel like the behaviour of an unscrupulous leader. And it probably is. But leaders who have a lot at stake in the successful outcome of taking an organization forward will sometimes go to any lengths to achieve their aims. Some leaders take the view that they are likely to upset some people in their endeavour anyhow and this is a natural consequence of achievement.

In the end, it is a gamble. And leaders use their instinct and intuition at all times to weigh up whether a risk is worth taking and what are the likely outcomes.

Remember that leaders are not regarded as 'nice people' by everyone.

Appreciation

A leader can influence people to stay on course in delivering the vision by expressing appreciation at regular intervals. If a leader asks an organization to take on a difficult mission, then it is extremely important to express gratitude at several points along the way. Good Implementation leaders use 'Appreciation Events' all the time to continue to motivate and influence people to continue on the journey.

16. *I am certain we will get there*

Strong leaders act with confidence and certainty: confidence that they are the right person to lead the organization and certainty that the vision they are pursuing will be achieved.

Confidence

I believe in my ability to lead the organization.

Confirmation

Progress confirms that I have chosen the right path.

Certainty

I believe that the future state is better and it can be reached.

No one can really know the future and leaders have no special skills to see the future and how it will evolve. But they <u>behave</u> as though they know the future. What is key here is that leaders <u>believe</u> in their vision and that it will happen.

As time progresses a leader accumulates information which will give them an insight to the outcome. Events along the way will contribute to the insight. Assumptions that were established at the start will either prove to be valid or invalid. Obstacles are overcome and progress confirms that the vision can be achieved.

We can view the journey in the following way:

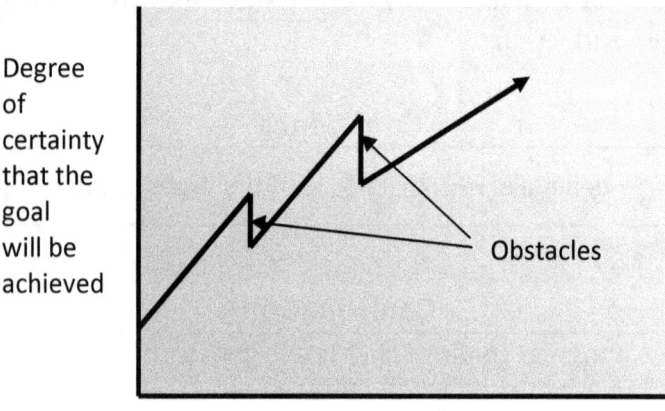

Time

Obstacles occur which impact the probability of success. But as these are overcome, then the probability of success increases again. Obstacles may result in a modification to the vision but a leader will continue to evaluate the value of the final goal and determine if it represents progress.

Why is belief is so important?

Leaders depend on the input of a lot of people to make the organizational vision a reality. Some of these may be passive investors looking for a return on their investment. It is vital that the leader projects confidence and certainty so that the investor will continue to have faith in the outcome.

Leaders sit at the top of the organization and are in constant communication with all the key players and teams. This gives a leader a unique view of how the organization is performing. In reality, no one else has this view.

The leader has the ability to digest all the information and confirm that the organizational goal can still be achieved. The leader must constantly communicate their perspective to the organization as a whole. The wider organization trusts that the leaders are using all the information they have to re-evaluate the design and implementation plans and confirm their belief that the organization is on target to achieve the goal.

Communicating behaviours of confidence and certainty

Leaders must communicate often and effectively. The effectiveness of the communication will almost entirely depend on the message itself and integrity with which it is delivered. Leaders should ensure that updates related to organizational progress cover all aspects of the vision, design and implementation. Has the vision been modified? Is the strategy still appropriate? Have there been obstacles and have they been overcome? Is the implementation on schedule? Will the benefits still be realized?

Integrity in delivering the message is vital to keeping the organization motivated. Any sense the issues are being 'covered up' or that the 'full truth' is not being revealed can easily come out in the behaviour of the leader when communicating. Not to communicate at all can create just as much uncertainty as to communicate insufficiently and dishonestly.

Leaders will be respected for their honesty. If there is a problem, say so. The difficulty for leaders is that most do not like to outline a problem without putting forward a solution. And not to put forward a solution could indicate a weakness – something that leaders really do not like.

Leaders who speak with confidence and passion are very effective in delivering sincere messages. You will see the leader use a lot of hand gestures, coupled with the raising and lowering of the tone and volume, looking directly at people in their audience. Often it is the sincerity of the message that convinces the audience just as much as the content itself.

Decisiveness and staying the course

Decisiveness is not entirely about the ability to make a decision, but it is also about the belief in the outcome of a decision. The belief that the outcome will happen will cause leaders to stay on the course as outlined in the design and implementation plans.

The organization may see obstacles as events that have the potential to derail the train. Leaders can anticipate obstacles and have contingency plans in place to overcome them. As such, they continue on the course in the knowledge that the goal can still be achieved.

Even if an obstacle is unforeseen, leaders assess the situation quickly and use their innovation skills to design ways around the problem. This is particularly true for design and Implementation leaders.

Blindness

If a leader learns that the vision cannot be realized, this can lead to a crisis of reputation and integrity. No leader likes to be associated with failure and often a leader will do everything to avoid failure, or at least the failure being attributed to them as individuals.

Some leaders continue the journey in the vain hope that a miracle can happen. It usually doesn't.

Some leaders continue in the hope that they can attribute the failure to someone else or to some event. Deflecting the accountability rarely works and in time the organization will see the truth.

The risk of damage to their reputation is so significant that a leader can blindly pursue the impossible. You need only look at the fall of some political leaders in the course of history to see this. Equally, it can play out in business and other institutions of society in the same way.

The best course for a leader who sees that the vision cannot be realized is come clean and communicate quickly and honestly. There is always the chance that the organization will retain some respect for a leader who tried, but did not make it. In the end, leaders are people who would rather try and fail, than not try at all.

17. Reaching the Promised Land, but is it any better?

So a day will hopefully come when the organization achieves its goal and the vision is realized.

But does it represent progress?

It is typical for a great celebration to take place when the vision is realized. And it is worth celebrating. Undoubtedly a lot of people will have put a big effort into achieving the goal. Their efforts must be recognized. Equally, reaching an organizational milestone is worth celebrating. Not every organization that sets out on a journey will get there.

But let us not forget that reaching the goal does not necessarily represent progress. We can only celebrate progress after a period of evaluation has occurred and any progress is measured in real terms.

Progress can be represented by an increase in sales, a reduction in costs, the cure of a disease, the winning of a trophy and so on. While some visions can measure success instantly, most take time. Many visions <u>do</u> represent progress, but some do not.

Measuring success

All success must be measured in a way that we can compare the initial state of the organization with the new state. If the new state is better, then the organization has increased its overall value. Value is the key ingredient that enables an organization to survive and develop. Value is measured in terms of an organization's ability; for example, the ability to generate additional profit from a new product.

In commercial terms, this can be quite easy as most companies measure their activity for accounting and financial management purposes anyhow. So the launch of a new product or the expansion into a new marketplace or the reduction in production costs can easily be seen in the Profit & Loss statement. But if the goal was to increase customer satisfaction or employee satisfaction, then the leaders must measure these through surveys and demonstrate progress clearly after a period of sufficient time has elapsed.

Success can easily be measured prematurely. I am sure that Sony celebrated the technological achievement of the Betamax video player/recorder and that Microsoft celebrated the launch of Windows Vista. Over time, neither were regarded as a success.

Reach the Future State → Creation of Value → Ability to Survive

Casualties along the way

The D-Day invasion of Northern France resulted in many casualties. But the military leaders knew this was probable and continued with the mission regardless.

Casualties in the pursuit of an organizational goal can and do happen. Leaders know this and few missions result in a situation where there are no casualties. Casualties can manifest themselves in the form of reputational damage, loss of key resources and people, creating an opportunity for a competitor, and so on.

Low-cost airlines may be among the most successful airlines in the world when measured by sales volume. But some low-cost airlines have sacrificed customer satisfaction in the process of becoming successful as measured by sales volume alone.

Failure to reward key people in the pursuit of a goal can cause them to leave and join a competitor. Having reached the future state, key resources and capabilities will still be required to sustain and develop the organization further. Competitors can easily imitate your new and innovative product and present a major threat to your sales potential. Long and expensive court battles may be the only way to protect your position, but these consume many of the organization's key resources and deflect them from building the next vision.

18. Building on success

Once an organization reaches its goal and determines that success has been achieved, the next step is to build on that success and protect the achievement.

This can be difficult.

If all the resources have been consumed in reaching the goal, there may be few resources left to develop onwards from the new state.

A company may launch a new product and be so overwhelmed with orders that it is unable to fulfil them in any meaningful time frame. Customers become impatient and competitors produce imitations, causing sales to drop.

Perhaps, after launching a new product, there is a high demand and sales increase significantly. After a few months, the product is found to have defects and many are returned for repair or replacement under warranty. The business is spending a lot of time and money carrying out the repairs and the reputation of the product is hit badly. Sales ultimately fall.

A business can go bust if it is unable to sustain the position of progress that it has achieved.

A medical advance must be capable of curing many people by building on the success of curing the first person.

A team that wins the league cannot afford to get relegated to a lower division in the subsequent season.

Success creates an expectation that further success is possible and leaders must incorporate strategies for sustainability when developing a vision for the organization.

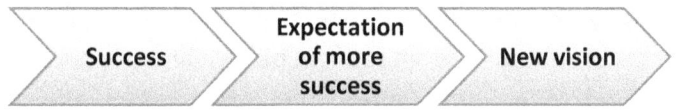

Strategies for sustainability

1. Protecting the asset

When the future state has been reached, the organization acquires a new asset and creates new value. Products, a relationship, intellectual property, a status in the community – all are good examples.

The asset must be protected in order to build a new vision and sustain the organization. Protection can come in the form of a copyright or patent and the leadership should not wait until the goal has been achieved before starting this process.

Retaining the expertise is a common form of protecting the asset. The same expertise that helped an organization get to where it is today will often be required to get the organization to its next destination.

2.   Reward and Recognition

Reward and recognition is the most important first step that leaders take to retain the expertise in the organization. Leaders create incentives for key resources to achieve the goal, but create further incentives to retain these people for the next generations of organizational goals. Be careful not to let this can lead to the concept of the 'golden handcuffs', whereby key people are retained by extraordinarily generous rewards and subsequent performance is poor.

Recognition is just as important as reward and particularly so in some cultures of the world – most notably those in Asia. Recognition elevates the status of a person in their community and among their peers. The achievement of the organization is linked directly to a person and they wear a 'badge of honour'. Some organizations have a 'Hall of Fame' where photographs of key achievers hang proudly.

3.   Conservation of resources and capabilities

Resources and capabilities are the fuel that drives an organization forward and no organization can run on an empty tank. The strategy must allow for the conservation of resources and capabilities to build and develop the new state. A strategy cannot consume all resources in the 'getting there' phase and leave nothing to develop the organization further.

Most people who buy a new car can afford to run it. They have already figured out the cost of fuel, insurance, maintenance and so forth. Equally, Design leaders must ensure that when the future state has been reached, the organization can afford to keep it.

The cost of maintaining the future state can be high and is typically measured in terms of the commitment required of people, cost of working capital, stock, raw materials and political support.

4. Leadership beyond the vision

It should not be assumed that leaders who take an organization to a future state have the ability to take the organization forward again. Leaders who sustain, protect and grow an organization can be quite different to the leaders who create visions of a new future state.

Leaders can be aligned to certain types of vision. Some leaders are best suited to new and innovative products, while other leaders are best suited to increasing value from additional sales through expansion into new markets. Leaders have tenure and it is important to recognise that there will be a time for a leader to step aside and let someone new take over.

5. <u>Conveyor belt of visions</u>

Organizations must have a conveyor belt of visions:

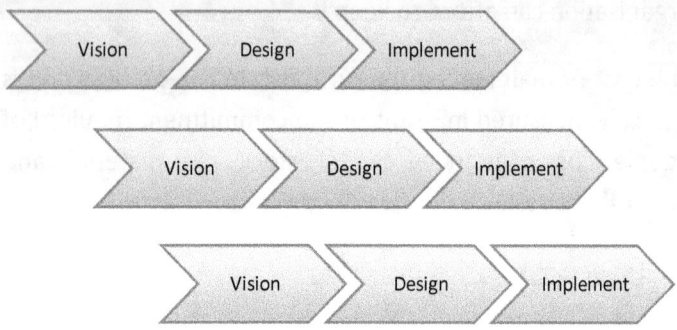

While the current vision is coming to a conclusion, the next vision should be well under way and even more should be in the stages of formation. Whatever success is attained in a vision will be short lived and an organization must be ready to develop the next vision in order to sustain and grow. The rate at which a new vision is developed will differ from organization to organization. For example, Mercedes-Benz generally bring out a new version of existing models every 6 to 7 years, while others enhance their model every 3 to 4 years. Different organizational strategies are at play in these situations.

6.   Roll over the team and throw away the golden handcuffs

Retaining expertise in the organization is a valid strategy. But golden handcuffs have the potential to retain behaviours and approaches that could become outdated. When this happens, it can be very difficult to replace the current team – even if this becomes necessary for the organization to survive.

An organization must turn over its people. There are no set rules to this, but it should typically be between 7.5% and 10% per year. Less than 5% typically means that the organization might stagnate by becoming entrenched in a single style and may be unable to make the necessary changes required to survive and develop. New thinking, new approaches and new skills must come to every organization over time. If the rate of turnover is more than 20%, this can cause the expertise to walk out the door before the organization has fully utilized their capability.

Let us suppose that an organization now faces stiff competition in a market which they have dominated for many years. The current resources might be predominately experts in manufacturing and delivery but competitors have sourced the manufacturing at cheaper, more efficient locations and are gaining market share by focusing on a slick marketing campaign. Leaders must be willing to acquire a completely new set of expertise in order to challenge the competition. Golden handcuffs mean that existing resources will not leave and remain in the company focused only on their own way of doing things – a way that the organization no longer needs. I am not suggesting that people should be fired because the landscape changes, I am suggesting that people need to be re-equipped with new skills and the organization must bring in expertise it does not have – but really needs.

If an organization has rewarded people in the past for achieving sales volume and now wants to reward people for innovation, the golden handcuffs have to be thrown away or at least replaced with a different set.

19. Bringing calm after the change

Reaching a goal means a new state for an organization. And this means that organizations go through a period of change along the journey.

Many people do not like change. But change is necessary and it is important for leaders to establish calm and order in the new state. This must be carried out with some degree of haste which is balanced by empathy to those who struggle with change. Time is not on a leader's side because the next organizational goal is in the rear view mirror.

Leaders who bring their organization to a future state can help the organization cope with the changes that the future state brings by taking on some key activities:

Communicate

Be first to deal with change

Give everyone a part to play

Spend time with people

Listen, listen, listen

Communicate

Leaders must explain the purpose of change and why it is necessary for organizational growth and survival. Once the goal is achieved, leaders must do everything to continually reassure people that the change is beneficial. Repeated communications enforce the message. It usually takes two to three deliveries for people to absorb the message.

Be first to deal with change

If a leader is asking people to accommodate change, they themselves must be the first to adopt the change. This is essential to leadership integrity and can often be overlooked.

A leader who asks an organization to become more efficient and increase productivity must demonstrate these principles in their own behaviour. In difficult economic environments elected members of a government must curtail their personal benefits if they intend to ask the population at large to accept an increase in taxes.

Give everyone a part to play in change

People feel comfortable with change if they have an active part to play in bringing about change. This is particularly important where a person's role is not as critical to the organization in the future state than it is in the current state.

Bringing an organization to a future state can place greater emphasis on some areas and less emphasis on others. If distribution is outsourced, then those who played a key role in distribution in the past will feel less important in the future. Leaders must explain the need for the change and try to position people where their level of contribution is retained – even if this results in a different type of contribution. Retraining people with new skills is often an essential part of re-establishing people's level of contribution.

Spend time with small groups of people

Leaders can often be seen as people in elevated positions who have little involvement in the day-to-day business of the organization. Unfortunately, this is true is so many organizations.

Leaders should spend at least one hour every week with a random selection of people across the organization. These 'Meet the Boss' meetings should not include members of the management team, but could include one or two members of the leadership team. There should be no agenda and it should not turn exclusively into a 'Questions for the Boss' session. It should be informal and include refreshments and discuss any matter that is put on the table by any attendee.

These sessions can help a leader identify the concerns and issues of the organization – particularly in a time of change. Undoubtedly many questions will be put forward by attendees, but leaders must be willing to ask for suggestions, hear them out and follow up by validating them.

People must feel that they have contributed to the development of the organization and giving people a forum to make suggestions is very healthy for an organization.

Listen, Listen, Listen

Leaders cannot presume that they hold a monopoly on ideas and must be willing to listen to what people have to say. Not giving people the opportunity to express their opinion, or ignoring it once it is expressed, can alienate a leader from their organization. Not every suggestion put forward will be practical and individuals may not have the full organizational perspective to understand why their suggestion may not work. But some will be worth considering and a leader must listen to these.

Leaders deal with change more than most people and are typically capable of accommodating change easier than others. Leaders must recognise that most people can take longer to adjust to new circumstances. Patience is required by leaders, who need to spend time listening and guiding people through the period of change.

The pace of change accelerates as the implementation phase gets under way and it is at this point that leaders must spend more time with people in the organization. Visionary leaders should begin to include Design and Implementation leaders in communication sessions as soon as the goal starts to become visible in the distance.

20.   I think I know myself, or do I...

Leaders must be fully aware of their own personality, leadership characteristics and ability.

This awareness must be complete and viewed with honesty. A leader who lacks a true awareness of their ability could potentially miscalculate where they need the help of others. This could lead to significant gaps in the overall ability of the leadership team and impact their ability to succeed.

Most people think they know themselves and many times I have heard people reading their 'character profile' and say "yes, that sounds like me." This can be easy to do when looking at your strengths, but is a lot more difficult to do when looking at your weaknesses.

In general, leaders have more strengths than weaknesses and as a simple rule of thumb I would propose that a leader's ability to lead comes from 80% of their character, while those attributes that stand in the way of success come from the other 20%. Or put it another way, you should be able to describe four leadership strengths about yourself for every gap.

If you ask a colleague to describe your strengths, they will typically find this task easier than describing your weaknesses. However difficult it is, you must find a person whom you trust that can help you understand your strengths and your weaknesses.

Now some leaders are entirely uncomfortable with the use of the term 'weakness'. Some leaders believe that weakness is not compatible with leadership. I would challenge this. To err is human. We all make mistakes and leaders are no exception.

I am using the term 'weakness' in the context of leadership to mean a characteristic that has the potential to impact a leader's performance in achieving their goal, nothing more than that. There are two key areas where a leader's character can bring out a strength or weakness and it is vital that every leader looks in the mirror and understands these:

> **1. Interaction with people**

> **2. Personal characteristics**

The objective is to know where your strengths and weaknesses are and <u>manage</u> them appropriately.

If you find it difficult to interact with certain types of people, there is a danger that in meetings with such people you may come into conflict with them. This can stand in the way of influencing them – and they may be critical to achieving the goal. Once you know about yourself, you can be more 'managed' in your approach.

If you are the type of person that loves admiration, then it is important that you manage your behaviour in a way that you are seen to share the accolades rather than harbour them for yourself.

Interaction with people

Leaders interact with many people. These interactions are critical to influencing people to play their part in achieving the vision. Personalities differ and a leader cannot expect to 'connect' positively with everyone. However, a leader should know the type of people that they have difficulty interacting with and manage their behaviour accordingly. This really has nothing to do with what is 'right' and what is 'wrong'; it is fundamentally about how a leader behaves.

For example, many leaders might find it difficult to work with an investor who constantly questions the plans to achieve the vision and seeks constant updating, with high levels of detail. Whether the investor is right or wrong for asking is not important. What is important is how a leader behaves towards the investor. In this example, the leader must remember that the investor's investment might be critical to the overall goal. To show reluctance to provide the information might send the wrong message to the investor and cause them to reduce or even withdraw their support.

Behaviours that leaders use to improve their human interaction include the following:

- Be patient and understanding with a person – for whatever reason.

- Offer deference and esteem to a person who places a high level of importance on hierarchies.

- Engage in a social connection outside the work environment as a means of 'getting to know each other'.

- Interact on the same level through appropriate language and terms that relate to the people's understanding and knowledge.

Personal characteristics

Everyone has some personality characteristics which may cause other people to like or dislike them. It is also worth noting that one person may find a characteristic admirable while another person may dislike it.

It is important that a leader understands enough about themselves to identify aspects of their personality which have the potential to contribute to, or limit, their ability to be a successful leader. Again, this is not a matter of 'right' or 'wrong', it is about your behaviour.

Common characteristics found in a leader include:

- Sensitivity. Can you be sensitive to other people's needs and views?

- Honesty. Are you able to communicate with others in a way that they feel you are not hiding anything?

- Courtesy. Can you be courteous to people?

- Accountable. Are you able to take full responsibility for the organization you are leading?

- Loyalty. Can you remain loyal to the organization?

- Enthusiasm: Can you show eagerness when someone makes a suggestion – regardless of how effective it might be?

- Open-mindedness: Are you capable of being receptive and interested in the opinions and ideas of others?

- Self-control: Can you manage your actions, words and expressions appropriately and without making people feel uncomfortable?

- Encouragement. Can you express your thoughts in a way that motivates and encourages others?

- Adaptability. Can you adjust your behaviours according to the situation?

- Conscientious. Can you keep a high level of focus despite the challenges?

- Industriousness. Are you interested and capable of taking on any task in order to support the team?

- Care. Can you execute tasks with due care and attention?

- Compassion: Can you empathize with the difficulties that others find themselves in?

- Dedication. Can you remain committed to the organizational goals?

- Endeavour to win. Are you able to focus entirely on a positive outcome?

- Patience. Can you remain composed when people and events do not move forward as you expect?

- Perfectionism. Do you strive to achieve an outcome with the highest level of success?

- Bravery. Are you willing to pursue a goal in spite of serious obstacles and even in the light of your own personal fear?

- Decisiveness. Are you able to make decisions in a timely manner and with a high degree of confidence and determination?

- Drive. Can you pursue a goal with a high degree of energy?

- Perseverance. Are you willing to continue working towards a goal and overcome obstacles?

- Composure. Can you remain strong in the face of overwhelming difficulties?

- Stable. Can you remain committed to your strategy?

- Passion. Do you pursue goals with excitement and zeal?

As everyone is different, you will possess these characteristics in a variety of different levels. The combination that you have is likely to be unique and cause you to behave in a certain way when faced with a given situation. These behaviours can have a positive effect or a negative effect depending on the emotion they bring out. Positive emotions such as happiness and joy will be greeted well by the organization while negative emotions such as anger and fear will not.

If you are a person who strives for perfection and you find that some people get the job done but it is not to a standard that you would like, then you could become annoyed or angry at them. If you are a person who finds it difficult to show compassion, then you may become bitter and annoyed when a key person is missing because of a personal circumstance that you find difficulty empathising with.

Leaders should remember that different people have the potential to view the same characteristics in either a positive or negative way. For some people, bravery may be a noble pursuit and even necessary to achieve an organizational goal. For others, bravery without due care can be viewed as a reckless effort which could cause damage to you and the organization's reputation.

Leaders should examine carefully the list of characteristics and understand the extent to which they describe your personality and behaviour. If your behaviour limits your ability to be a successful leader then you must make <u>deliberate behavioural adjustments</u>.

Your character will most likely cause you to behave in an 'automatic' way. Without even thinking, you might find yourself responding to a given situation according to an emotion that has been triggered by your character. Leaders need to make a deliberate effort to control their behaviour if it has the potential to be damaging.

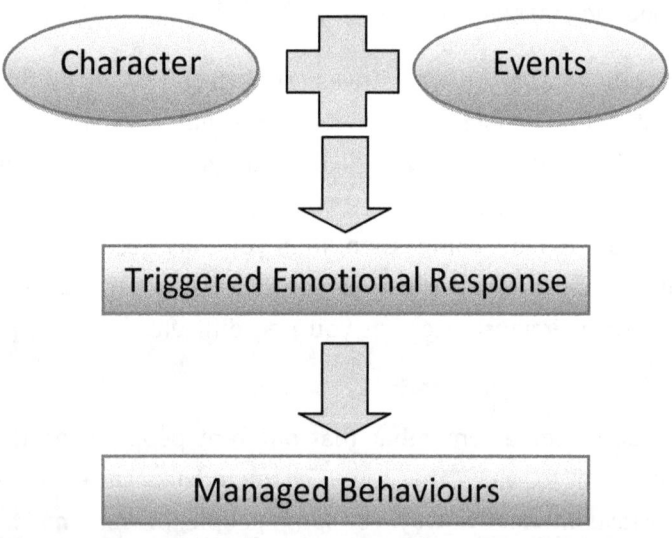

Let us take an example to explore this concept further.

Let us suppose that you are a leader of an organization and one member of your leadership team is an outstanding creative and innovative thinker. You decide to bring them on to the leadership team because they have the potential to significantly add to the strategic planning for the organization. However, the person in question can sometimes lack drive – particularly when they feel that they are not getting enough praise and recognition. At one particular meeting you observe this person sitting quietly and not contributing to a key discussion on strategy. This event triggers an emotional response in you. The emotion of anger. Based on an understanding of your character you try to manage your behaviour. Instead of openly berating the person, you decide to take them to one side and discuss the issue – calmly. If the person fails to respond, you can then take decisive action.

Situations like this present themselves every day and it can be very difficult to adjust your behaviour against the grain of what feels natural for your character and personality.

You can use one element of your character to balance another. For example, let us suppose that you are being interviewed for a magazine and there is a constant stream of questions which aim to undermine your dedication. By contrast, you may feel that you spend many long hours on the project and the last thing you were lacking was dedication. Some people are likely to become annoyed and angry in this situation. However, if your character is one where patience and calmness are a strength, then you can deliberately manage your response.

Managing behaviours is difficult and can feel like you are asking yourself to do something that is entirely unnatural.

The importance of understanding yourself in terms of characteristics, emotions, and behaviours cannot be underestimated. They are fundamental parts of how you interact with people and are integral to how you influence and motivate others.

It is important to stress that managing your behaviours is only required when you behave in a way that seriously impacts your ability to inspire people to follow you as a leader.

Managing your behaviours draws upon your judgement and instinct on how to behave in a given situation. There is a time to be calm and there is a time to be angry.

21. Aiming to be a better leader

Leaders should constantly look to develop their skills and improve their leadership capability. Aiming to be a better leader is a quest that all leaders should pursue. Being a good leader is not a state that you arrive at, it is a goal that you must constantly aspire to.

Leadership differs from other pursuits because there is little or no room for mistakes. It can be a 'one strike and you're out' game. You rarely get a second chance to be a leader.

Leadership capability is derived from the combination of the following:

- Intellectual capability

- Experience

- Characteristics of your personality

Academic capability is a combination of the intellectual ability of a person and the knowledge they acquire over time. Once a person reaches maturity, their intellectual ability will remain relatively static for many years (depending on their overall health and well-being). The ability to solve problems and make decisions is at the core of a person's intellectual ability and while it can be improved and developed through exercise of the mind, it cannot be substantially enhanced. The point at which maturity is reached will, of course, vary from person to person.

By contrast, knowledge can be accumulated throughout the course of a person's life. For many people, knowledge is built up through the process of education, observation and natural inquisitiveness. Once formal education is completed, a person continues to build their store of knowledge through ongoing study, tuition, coaching and mentoring.

Knowledge can also be accumulated through experience. In fact, many people would argue that the only true way to know something is to experience it. For example, you will probably learn a great deal more about a country by going and living there than by reading books.

Finally, the characteristics of your personality will significantly contribute to your ability to be a leader. These are part of you as a person and enable you to use judgement, intuition and so on.

It is not possible to substantially add or subtract from your intellectual capability or the characteristics of your personality as these are built in to you as a person. In order to develop your leadership capability, you must focus predominately on the things that you can develop and control. These include the following:

1) Your ability to acquire knowledge through learning

2) Your ability to acquire wisdom from experience

3) Your ability to manage your behaviours

Constant focus on the aspects of your leadership capability that you can develop and enhance will give you a better chance of being a good leader. Therefore it is important to look for a good mentor, learn from the experience of success and error, study and read books, observe what others do, how they do it and why they do it, understand the characteristics of your personality and learn how to manage your behaviours.

We can build a topography which captures the capability of a leader and begin to examine the ways in which a leader can develop further.

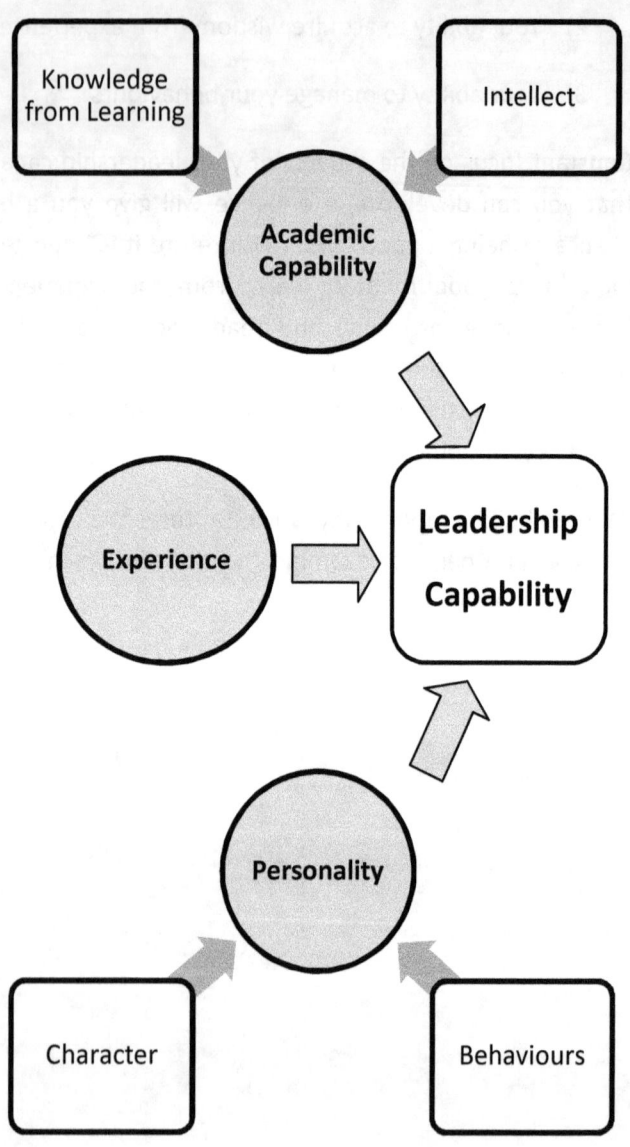

Knowledge from learning

Learning can be achieved in a number ways:

- Formal education

- Workplace tuition

- Personal study

- Observation

- Experience

Formal education typically takes place up to the age of 25 to 30 years and for the most part it is completed <u>prior</u> to starting a career. Many people pursue additional education later on as a supplement.

Learning continues through the process of self-study and workplace tuition and many organizations have programmes of personal development for their staff. Continuous study should be a part of every leader's routine. Education allows a leader to learn about concepts and ideas and there is a constant flow of new ideas – especially about leadership!

Learning from observation and experience

But all types of education and tuition cannot provide the real knowledge acquired through observation and experience. Observing how leaders behave in a real situation and being part of a leadership team making real decisions is the most beneficial form of learning.

There comes a point when a leader's experience outweighs their academic qualification. Think of the last time you had an interview for a job. How much time was spent discussing your qualifications and how much time was spent discussing your experience? More than likely you spent much more time discussing your experience.

Observing leaders in action is easy. Watch the daily news and the chances are that many items will centre on decisions made by leaders and the consequences of these decisions. Look locally to your own community and its many clubs and societies. Look for clear signs of vision, design and implementation in action.

As time passes, your ability to learn from observation and experience will increase. Reflection allows you to ponder and review what happened, why it happened and what could have happened if different decisions had been made. Many things that were difficult to see at the time they occurred become easy to see after a period of reflection has passed.

In this way, reflection leads to a sense of wisdom.

You may have heard the expression that 'it is easy to be wise after the event' but it would probably be more accurate to say that 'it is easy to be wise after reflection.'

Wisdom is the ability to discern and gain insight from an experience from which you have gained knowledge.

Remember that it takes time to reflect and acquire wisdom.

Managing your behaviours

We have previously discussed how events can trigger an automatic emotional response and how it is necessary to manage your behaviours as a leader.

Understanding your character and personality and what triggers emotional responses takes time and significant introspection. Learning how to manage your behaviours can yield significant benefits. If a certain type of behaviour or event makes you angry and that anger leads you to make inappropriate actions, then learn how to manage the behaviours that you respond with and you will significantly improve your ability to interact with others.

Using judgement to manage your behaviours is essential. For example, you might get angry if someone does not clean up after spilling coffee on their table and decide to manage your behaviours by politely asking them to attend to it. But if someone upsets a customer and your organization looses a large sale, then you might feel that something a bit stronger that a polite discussion is called for!

Having a mentor and discussing your behaviours is a very good way to learn about yourself. The more you know about yourself, the better are the chances of becoming a good leader.

22. Political alliances

When most people think of politics it is likely to be in the context of political regimes, philosophies and parties that compete for power to govern a country. But politics plays a role in almost every dimension of society, from families to charities to local town councils to universities to religious groups to business and, of course, in government.

Politics can be basically described as the way people are influenced to make a collective decision for an entire organization. A political alliance is a group of people who share a common view of where an organization should go and their aim is to influence the decision makers to take the necessary steps towards that goal.

There are two key reasons why politics is of importance to leaders:

1. Leaders form political alliances to influence people to support their vision.

2. Leaders can be subject to influence by political alliances.

Organizational structures are typically hierarchical in nature, with a single leader sitting at the top of the pyramid. Below the leader is the leadership team, the management team and the individual members of the organization itself.

In contrast to this vertical structure of an organization, a political alliance can be composed of people at any level. Political alliances can also function outside the organization and can significantly impact the ability of an organization to achieve its goals.

Let's take a look at some key aspects of politics that leaders should be aware of:

Awareness

It sounds simple, but it can be remarkably surprising how many leaders are not aware of the political alliances in the organization and how the dynamics of these groups evolve over time. People can keep their 'membership' of an alliance quiet and wait until the appropriate time to express their opinion. In this way, an alliance can operate at a sub-organizational level and its very existence can remain relatively unknown.

Leaders need to have a strong network within the organization in order to be aware of the various alliances and their objectives. Leaders should give sufficient time to form their own view about these objectives and whether they should support, compromise or oppose them.

Eventually, members of a political alliance will attempt to influence others towards their viewpoint. At this point, the political alliance emerges from the sub-organizational level and into the mainstream. It is essential to avoid being surprised by this and to have your own position thought out thoroughly in advance. The element of surprise can place an alliance in a position of strength and those who are unaware of their existence can feel isolated and even threatened.

Why did an alliance begin?

A leader should ask why a group of like-minded individuals felt the need to form an alliance in the first place. If the alliance behaves in a secretive way, what does this say about the freedom of expression at the leadership and management level of an organization?

Alliances can be healthy and it is good to see people discussing matters of organizational importance among themselves. It is also good to see people attempting to influence decision makers. Leaders should encourage people to express opinions in a constructive manner and be open to new approaches. When a leader becomes closed to new ideas and concepts, alliances go underground. Underground alliances can be destructive as they attempt to question the leadership's ability to succeed and can significantly impact motivation.

Face off

If a leader does not support the change being proposed by a political alliance, there will be a face off. Even in a position where a leader is outnumbered, they should remain loyal to their convictions. Organizations are not democracies and the Organizational leader usually holds ultimate authority.

Leaders who oppose the position of a political alliance need to do so with justifiable cause. It is critical to state in a rational and logical way why you are taking your position and, above all, do not personalize it. Leaders who act on their instinct and judgement should say so. After all, this is a key capability of a leader, so do not be afraid to say that this is the basis of your decision.

Reach out to those in the alliance and ensure to keep the dialogue going.

Compromise

There are few situations where the objectives of a political alliance have no merit – at all. In fact, many have very creative ideas and should be given a lot of consideration!

In general, both parties should be willing to go through a phase of negotiation in which a compromise is the ultimate outcome. Organizational leaders have overall accountability and should only make changes if they believe that the organization will benefit from the proposal. A leader who makes changes for any other reason is taking significant risk and side-stepping their own intuition and judgement.

Compromise is good provided it is based on rational debate. Compromise based on reciprocal favours (I will support your alliance if you support mine) is highly risky.

External politics

Organizational leaders may need to exert influence on key individuals and groups outside an organization in order to acquire vital levels of support. For example, a leader who wishes to build a new hotel will need the support of the planning authorities, tourist groups, environmental groups and so on. Attempting to influence external parties should be done with rational and logical arguments to support the case.

External parties should only expect their reward and recognition to come from the benefits that a successful outcome brings. Any form of personal reward has the potential to be regarded as corruption.

If a politician agrees to support the establishment of a new factory which creates employment, then that politician can only expect to be rewarded by the electorate in the next election. History is littered with attempts by leaders to influence external parties through bribery, coercion and blackmail. Although it is easy to say that such methods should be avoided, the fact is that many leaders find it difficult to resist the temptation. What the endgame brings in terms of success can be so rewarding for the organization and/or the individual leaders that every avenue will seem attractive. Offers of reciprocal support (such as financial donations) to a third party should be avoided, even if it is legal and considered the norm in your culture and society. The reason is that the third party will be influenced by the perceived benefit to themselves and may not make an impartial decision.

23. Values: what is really important

Everyone has a 'value system' which outlines the hierarchy of what is important to them. This usually begins with oneself, our partner/spouse, near family, extended family, friends, community, county and certain possessions. In addition to these are the principles that we live by and these might include success, health, financial stability, caring for others, caring for the environment and so on.

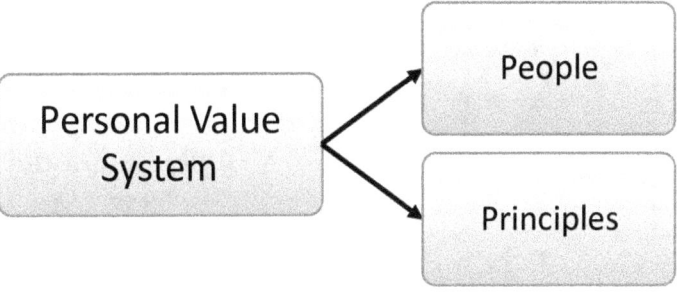

Leaders have a value system and it sets the standard for a set of behaviours that are expected in almost every situation. A leader's value system has its origins in their personal value system. Unlike a personal value system, which is restricted to an individual's life goals and behaviours, a leader's value system will impact the behaviour of everyone in the organization. The leader of an organization that places a value on the environment will expect everyone to limit the use of paper and recycle where appropriate. But an employee of such an organization may not practice these values outside of the work environment in their personal time.

A leader's value system will impact the standard behavioural model for an organization as well as strategies and implementation plans for future development.

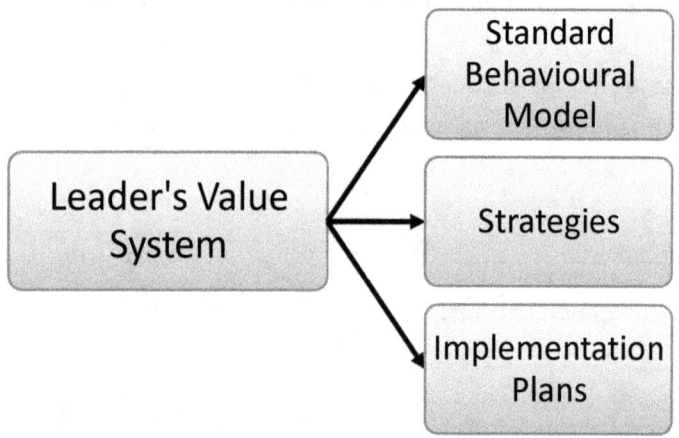

The value statement

We have seen that every organization will have a statement of vision and mission which outlines the future direction. Many organizations will also have a 'value statement' which sits side by side with the vision and mission statements.

Organizational value statements play a key part in both marketing the organization and attracting people with the right talent. The expression of values has the potential to create a cultural affinity with owners, customers, employees and other external parties with whom the organization has a relationship. Having a cultural affinity with an organization can motivate a person to contribute beyond the normal commitment that is expected. If an organization provides emergency relief in situations of man-made and natural disasters, it is highly likely that everyone who is involved has a strong cultural affinity with the organization and its aims.

Typical components of an organizational value statement would include the following:

- Customers. This would be expressed in a manner that suggests that providing a product or service that enables the highest level of customer satisfaction is the organization's highest priority.

- Quality of Product or Service. The organization aims to provide only the highest quality of product or service, with little or no defects.

- Employees. Many organizations explicitly place value on their workforce and express this in terms of providing people with meaningful assignments which are both personally fulfilling and financially rewarding. Opportunities for personal development and career advancement can also be found in these statements.

- Culture. This expresses the organization's values on behaviours and norms. It would outline areas such as innovation, approach to communication, professional behaviour and courtesy, conscientiousness, and so on.

- Ethical values. These include an expression of support by the organization for non-profit organizations and humanitarian ideals.

Standard behavioural model

The standard behavioural model defines the boundaries of what is expected from every member of the organization in the way they behave.

Behaviours can be classified as follows:

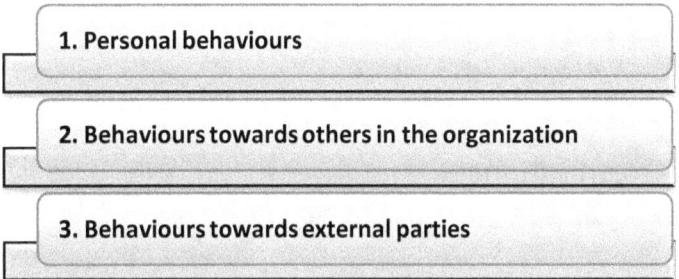

1. **Personal behaviours**

2. **Behaviours towards others in the organization**

3. **Behaviours towards external parties**

Personal behaviours refer to a person's attitude to personal matters such as dress code, tidiness, generosity, confidentiality and so on.

Behaviours towards others in the organization relate to what is acceptable when working as part of a team and covers all aspects of acceptable communication behaviour.

Behaviours towards external parties relates to how everyone is expected to behave towards customers, suppliers, and other parties with whom the organization has a relationship.

Organizations set a standard for all these behaviours and everyone is expected to adhere to them – even if a person does not have a natural tendency to do so! Behaviours say a great deal about an organization and can positively or negatively impact on an organization's image.

Strategies and the value system

Design leaders are tasked with defining the strategy for achieving the organizational goal. One of the key considerations in developing a strategy is the inclusion of the organizational values and the exclusion of approaches that contravene these values.

Consider the case of an organization that explicitly expresses its support for a 'fair trade' approach to purchasing materials to manufacture its products. A strategy to reduce costs by outsourcing the manufacturing must include careful evaluation of the cultural and ethical values of employees and suppliers. This should ensure that there is no conflict of values that could significantly harm the organization's integrity.

Many organizations have chosen to market their products and services almost entirely on the basis of their organizational values. In many cases, there is an additional cost associated with this strategy which often results in a higher price for the end product. Nonetheless, consumers who share the organizational value may be willing to pay a premium price in the knowledge that they are supporting a cause that they have a strong affinity towards.

Implementation plans and the value system

Having decided on the strategic use of resources and capabilities to achieve the organizational goal, Implementation leaders develop plans, design processes and establish teams to execute the strategy. Once again, the inclusion of organizational values will impact what is permissible and what should be excluded.

Consider the case of an organization that supports the conservation of energy and aims to reduce the environmental impact of the processes it uses to manufacture its products. Introducing a process that increases the productivity but also increases the consumption of energy per unit produced could be seen to be in conflict with the value system. This could happen in countries that experience high climatic temperatures and where there is a need to install energy-consuming air conditioning systems to manage the manufacturing environment.

24. Letting others lead

An organization can only have one leadership team comprising a small number of people who set a vision for a future state, design a strategy to reach the goal and implement the road to success.

The Organizational leader must be willing to allow each member of the leadership to lead and this must be done in accordance with their capability. There is a temptation in every leader to get personally involved in every initiative. While a reasonable level of participation is good, excessive involvement is unhealthy. There are two key reasons why leaders need to be balanced with their contribution:

1. Leaders must recognize that others may have higher levels of ability in some areas.

2. Leaders must allow others to develop their leadership skills and make meaningful contributions.

Consider a situation where the vision is to expand the business by leveraging existing capabilities and create a new product line. The Organizational leader asks two members of the leadership team to develop the strategy. Clearly these two people are Design leaders and this is probably their core expertise. The Organizational leader may have an outstanding ability to see that the new product line is the right organizational goal but may not be as talented in design and implementation. Therefore, they must be willing to let others lead the organization according to available skills and capabilities.

Outright 'Visionary leaders' and 'Owner/Leaders' can be tempted to get involved in design and implementation – even if the profile of the leadership team indicates that it would be better to let others take on this task. Participation is important, but not to the extent that others feel stifled. If a leader becomes overly involved in tasks that are best left to others then a sense that the leader does not trust the others to do the job right can easily emerge. This ultimately upsets the harmony in the team and people will not perform to their best.

Leaders must allow all members of the leadership team to make meaningful contributions to the vision, design and implementation of the organizational goals. This allows leaders to develop their skills and also allows future leaders to emerge. Obviously, if any member of the leadership team is not performing well, then it is the responsibility of the Organizational leader to take appropriate action.

Leaders are measured against the success of the overall goal and every member of the leadership team should feel a sense of achievement when the future state is reached.

25. Leadership in corporations

There are many situations where an organization is part of a larger entity and this creates a situation where there are two separate leadership teams:

1. Corporate leadership

2. Distributed organization leadership

For the purposes of illustration I will describe the overall organization in terms of a corporate core which connects to a series of distributed organizations.

The emergence of a globalized approach to business has seen a significant increase in multi-organizational entities. An early adopter of this model was the clothing industry. The 'corporate core' focused on developing visions and strategies for new products and established organizations across the globe to focus on mass-volume and low-cost manufacturing. This concept was subsequently copied by the technology industry and has been largely responsible for the proliferation of highly functional, low-cost technology devices such as smart phones, personal computers, personal music players, cameras, and so on. More and more industries utilize this approach including the motor car industry and the pharmaceutical industry

The core vision and strategy is determined by the corporate leadership team, while the distributed organizations are focused on implementing the roadmap and sustaining the achievement that the future state brings.

Distributed organizations bring unique value in terms of their cost, access to specific markets, tax benefits, specific types of skills, to mention but a few. The responsibility for overall organizational leadership lies with the leadership team at the corporate core. However, a leadership team will be required at each of the distributed organizations and in addition to their implementation role they will look to build on the unique value of the organization and enhance their overall contribution. This can lead to a situation where the distributed organization aims to develop a vision for itself while also contributing to the overall vision for the larger entity.

The pursuit of a vision for a distributed organization is entirely reasonable and should be supported and encouraged. However, it should be done in tandem with achieving the organization's overall goals and avoid any action in which these could be compromised.

Most of all, the organizational goal takes precedence over any goals of the distributed organization.

The profile of a multi-organizational entity looks like this:

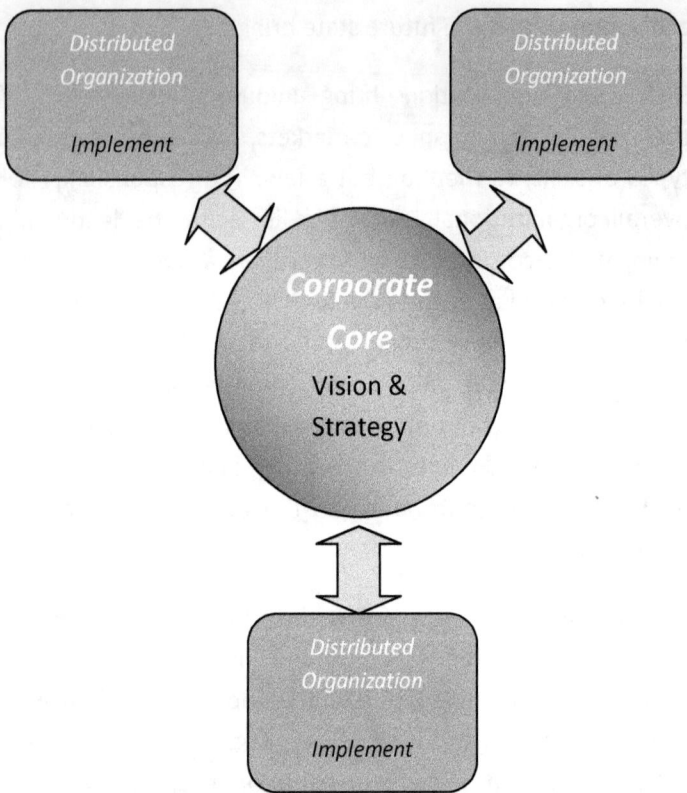

Corporate core

- Sets vision for the corporation. This will typically include decisions regarding the range of products and services as well as the marketplace that the business will focus on.

- Determines the appropriate strategy for achieving the goals of the business. This includes decisions regarding how and where key functions are performed such as research and development, product design, manufacture, marketing delivery and support.

Distributed organization

- Focused primarily on the implementation of the strategy and sustaining the position achieved by reaching the goals. The way in which the organization contributes will depend on the unique value that it brings. Their role can include product manufacture, product support, business support functions (HR, Finance, etc.), and product distribution.

Because the corporate core determines the role it wants the distributed organization to play, there is a potential for tension between the leadership of the two entities. The leadership team at the distributed organization will want to develop their own vision, design and implementation plans in order to contribute beyond the current role that they are being asked to fill. For example, they may feel that product manufacture alone limits their overall capacity to contribute.

Leadership at the distributed organization perform a duel leadership role:

1. Implementation of leadership for the corporation.

2. Vision, design and Implementation leadership for the distributed organization.

Let us look at some of the issues that this dilemma presents and how leadership teams in both entities can work together effectively.

Distributed organizations must fundamentally understand the primary reason for their existence. The corporate leadership has identified a unique value that the distributed organization brings and they are told to get on with it.

And so they should.

But any organization that does the same thing year after year is not growing and over time their unique value will be eroded. It is the responsibility of the distributed organizational leadership to develop a new value proposition and to convince the corporate core of the benefits this can bring. New and enhanced value propositions can often involve the distributed organization moving outside the role they are being asked to fill and into the role of the corporate core. Consider the example of an organization that is focused on product manufacture but wishes to move up in value by taking part in product design, which up to now has been the role of the corporate core.

Corporate leadership cannot limit the role of a distributed organization without understanding that such limitations could cause it to regress. So, they must specifically ask the distributed organization leadership to develop visions for their organization and be willing to listen to all proposals. Ultimately, the corporate leadership owns the overall vision, strategy and implementation roadmap and retains full power in deciding the role of a distributed organization.

Key areas of focus for the corporate leadership include:

- Ensuring the distributed organization understands the vision, strategy and implementation plans. But most of all, ensuring that they understand the role they are being asked to fill.

- Recognizing the dynamics of 'skills and knowledge' mobility. If competitors begin using their distributed organizations for product design, then that 'design capability' will become available in the marketplace. Such skills could be acquired to the benefit of the organization. Equally, the people at your distributed organization may be attracted to leave and join a competitor that they see is offering better opportunities for personal development.

- Redeploying some of the workforce when some functions move to a distributed organization. If some product support functions are moved to a distributed organization, then the people at the corporate core will need to be reassigned to new roles.

- Avoid a 'not invented here' culture. Some corporations believe that the corporate core is the only place that certain functions can be carried out to optimal effect. This can be a very dangerous position to take. Because of investments in education and the mobility of skills, no single location can claim to have a monopoly on any skill or capability. Many countries now have a highly talented workforce which can be utilized easily. Barriers to accessing this talent have also been removed and technology has allowed people to contribute effectively regardless of their location.

- Understanding 'capability clustering'. Over time, locations around the world have created clusters of capabilities. For example, Japan has been renowned for optics and miniaturization of electronics. Corporate strategies must understand the potential of these clusters when developing strategies to effectively utilize distributed organizations.

- Utilize the distributed organization leadership. Giving directives to leaders of distributed organizations has the potential to categorize them as 'order takers'. That is, they just follow orders and are not involved in any corporate strategy planning. Excluding them from such planning exercises limits their contribution and encourages a 'passive' behaviour rather than an 'active' behaviour.

- Interaction between distributed organizations. If several distributed organizations exist, then it is essential that they understand each other's role and unique value. Conflict can arise when two or more organizations try to contribute with the same value proposition. The corporate leadership has the responsibility to ensure that the strategy allows for effective and constructive use of each distributed organization. Competition between distributed organizations is healthy provided the outcome is beneficial to the corporation. Two organizations competing on the basis of cost cannot do so in a way that compromises the quality of the delivered product.

- One size does not fit all. Corporate strategies and implementation plans should respect the local culture of the distributed organization. This is particularly true where international and cultural boundaries exist between the corporate core and the distributed organization.

At a local level, the distributed organizational leadership must demonstrate their ability to establish a vision for the organization, design a strategy to achieve that vision and implement a roadmap to reach the future state. It will be critical to have a strong network in the corporate core and to be able to influence key decision makers.

Key areas of focus for the distributed leadership team include:

- Accept your primary mission. Be willing to accept the role that the corporation is asking you to do and respect their decision – even in situations where a corporate directive seems to contravene a previously agreed strategy. Your loyalty must be to the success of the organization, even at the expense of the distributed organization's own vision.

- Develop a reasonable vision for the organization. A vision that can be achieved in a reasonable time and is not in conflict with the corporate vision. A vision may need to be implemented in a series of incremental steps. It is not reasonable for a distributed organization to expect the transfer of all Research & Development from the corporate core to the local organization in a single step.

- Motivating the organization to contribute at its current level while trying to create new opportunities for people to contribute at a higher level. Many distributed organizations have a high turnover of staff because they restrict the capacity of people to develop by assigning them repetitive tasks.

- Build a connection to the business. Distributed organizations are often physically remote from the corporate core and many are located in a different country. Understandably, those who work at the corporate core have a strong sense of connection with the business. The corporate leadership is more visible as well as there being strong signs and symbols of corporate identity and success. In contrast, distributed organizations may be established in a location where there are few (if any) symbols of the corporation. In fact, the company's products may not even be sold in that region. Corporate leaders must frequently spend time at each distributed organization and communicate effectively regarding the vision and direction of the business. Equally, leaders at distributed organizations must help build the connection by doing regular communications, placing people on assignment, and running staff events in line with the rest of the corporation.

26. Leadership in a family business

Many organizations can trace their beginnings back to the ideas of one or two people. In the world of business, Arthur Guinness, Henry Ford, Bill Gates and Paul Allen are but a few.

It is reasonable that a person who starts a business would like their children to have a continued involvement in the business over time. Inasmuch as a child can reflect the personality of their parents, they want to be sure that the business will continue to reflect the principles and values of its founders.

Many organizations are run successfully by leaders who trace their roots back to the founders. But, there is no guarantee that the child of a successful leader will be a successful leader themselves.

I have previously stated that a leader's ability to be successful comes from their personality and characteristics as well as their personal development through experience and knowledge. Given that an individual's personality and characteristics have their origins in their parents, it is reasonable that the child of a leader should inherit some their parent's ability to become a leader.

Think of some leaders you know in business, science, politics, and so on. Now try to remember the names of their children that were equally successful. You may come up with some names, but you may find it even more difficult to think of the names of their grandchildren who were renowned as equally successful leaders.

The circumstances in which a leader is successful will change over time. The dynamics of change in one period of human development will be different to those in subsequent eras. A leader who created a vision for an organization in the 1970s may not be as successful in creating a vision in the 2010s. As a result, leaders have tenure and must be willing to step aside and allow a new leadership to emerge. If this new leadership mirrors the previous leadership then over time there is a risk that an organization will stagnate. New leadership should mean new vision. And new vision enables an organization to grow.

Leaders become leaders because of the ability to lead and not because they are the children of a leader. Every leader must be evaluated on their own merits.

The ultimate aim of an organization is to survive and develop. Nothing should stand in the way of this – not even the founder's personal wish that their son or daughter be the one who leads the organization forward.

27. Leadership in a small to medium-sized business

It can be difficult to describe what a small or medium-sized business looks like, but for the purposes of this discussion let me outline some characteristics:

- Original founder(s) runs the business

- Has anything from 10 to 100 employees

- Has been in business for 5 to 10 years

- Has one or two main products or services

- Moderately successful but is poised for growth

So how do the concepts of leadership apply for a typical small to medium-sized enterprise (SME)? Does it make sense to have a leadership team? What leadership skills matter most?

The frameworks, concepts and models of leadership apply to all organizations – regardless of size. So let's look at how some key ideas work in practice for an SME.

Vision, design and implementation

Many SMEs are so focused on getting the next sale that they can easily lose sight of what they are actually aiming to do as an organization. Many SMEs may not even have a three-year business plan. The business starts with an idea for a product or service and the initial goal may just be as simple as making it commercially viable. Sales start to build and the focus is almost entirely on fulfilment of orders and building a customer base.

Time can pass quickly and sooner or later the leaders will ask questions about the future direction for the business. What do they want the organization to be and what do they want the organization not to be?

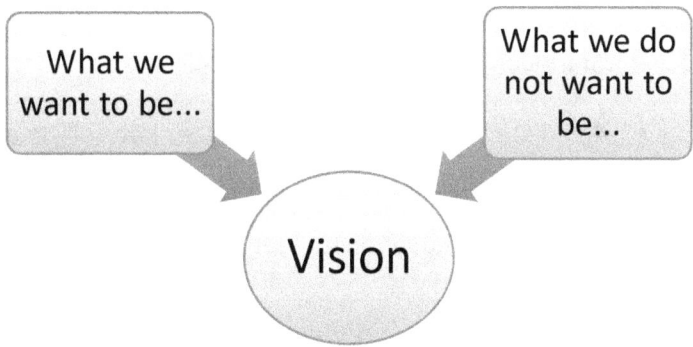

Defining a vision focuses the organization on the future and answers these questions. There may be some debate and discussion, maybe even some argument, but this can be constructive and once the outcome is a clear picture of the organization's goals, then it is worthwhile.

Vision must be accompanied by a design/strategy and an implementation plan. Because of their size, SMEs may have limited resources and capabilities and may have to be very creative in how they develop strategies and plans to achieve their goals.

The leadership team

It may feel somewhat inappropriate to have a management and a leadership team in an organization of say 20 people. Does it make sense to select three to five people from the organization and create a leadership team? The concept of a leadership team is still valid and many SMEs use a variety of approaches to build a leadership team:

- Start with a team of just three people.

- Appoint non-executive directors (i.e. non full-time employees).

- Identify retired business leaders who can act as advisors.

- Utilize external consultants and mentors.

- Meet every three months for a half day.

The sooner an organization establishes a leadership team, the better the chances of focusing on the future and making plans to get there.

Being a leader of an SME can be lonely. Perhaps there are few people (if any) in the organization who can validate your ideas. Having a leadership team gives tremendous support and encouragement to leaders.

External mentors can also act as 'validators' by acting as good sounding boards for leaders.

Creativity and innovation

Creativity and innovation are key elements in developing a small organization into a large organization. Once the initial product or service has been developed and some commercial success has been achieved, it is easy to focus purely on sales volumes and feel that innovation is not as important anymore.

In reality, creativity and innovation become even more important as leaders figure out how to transform a small business into a large business. Leaders of SMEs face greater challenges because they have limited resources and capabilities due to their size:

- They have fewer employees and may lack some of the capabilities necessary for advancement.

- They are unlikely to have extensive financial resources.

- They have limited time to invest in organizational development.

- They have limited ability to bring in external expertise.

- The threat from competitors with greater resources can be significant.

- They can easily get absorbed by the day-to-day operations of the business. It can feel like every decision – no matter how small – requires their input.

So leaders need to be very creative on how to maximize the use of the limited resources and capabilities at their disposal.

Taking risks

An SME must take risks in order to advance, but there is usually little scope for error. Making the wrong decision can be fatal. The leader of an SME must use all their powers of intuition and judgement to make the right choice about developing and advancing the organization.

Not to take a risk can be equally damaging and can lead to limited growth of an organization or even complete stagnation. While the organization moves forward slowly, competitors and other start-ups with apparently limitless resources can seem to move forward quickly. Leaders must trust their instinct and review strategies constantly with colleagues and advisors.

Being nimble

One key advantage of an SME is its ability to rapidly adjust its direction and strategy. While large organizations take time to make decisions, an SME can evaluate the options and conclude on a course of action very quickly. Resources can be deployed swiftly and as the pace at which an SME learns is very high, the capability is established rapidly. This can give an SME 'first mover advantage' and occupy a market segment before others even get started.

Similarly, in times of low economic activity, an SME can modify their day-to-day operations and run very economically and lean. Since not every business survives an economic recession, those who do have the opportunity to take a larger slice of the market.

Focus on structure and processes that are efficient and effective

SMEs must establish a basic organizational structure which clearly outlines the roles and responsibilities for everyone.

It may not seem appropriate to have a human resources manager in an organization of 20 people, but the function of managing human resources must be established. It might be more appropriate to have a part-time HR manager, or for the managing director to take on the function. Regardless, the function has to be managed. Similarly, standard processes must be established to answer the phone, take customer orders, fulfil orders, collect payments, and so on.

Processes must be efficient and effective and have alternatives if resources are absent for any reason. Processes in SMEs often evolve because things have been done in a certain way for a long time. But this does not necessarily mean it is the most effective way. Because of the agile nature of an SME, improving effectiveness and efficiency can be relatively easy to implement.

28. Into the unknown. Taking a risk...

To be a leader means that you will need to take risks.

The future is unknown and because leaders are focused on a vision of a future state there will always be an element of risk associated with reaching the destination and the expected benefits it brings. Leaders manage risk every day and make decisions that impact the ability of the organization to achieve its goals. The concept of risk in leadership is relatively simple but it is essential for leaders to understand it.

Risk has the potential to impact the investment that an organization makes in attempting to achieve a new vision. As a result, the probability of a successful outcome is affected.

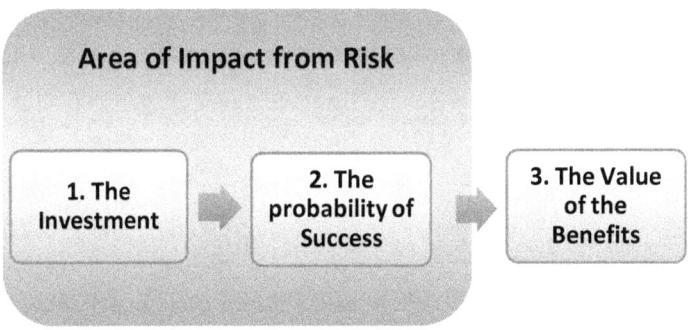

1.   The investment

Everything that an organization puts into achieving the goal of a future state can be regarded as the investment. All investments have their basis in the resources and capabilities of the organization.

Organizations will assign resources and capabilities into sustaining the existing position and for continued organic growth. This provides the organization with the ability to build additional resources and capabilities which will be needed to develop the next vision and/or mission.

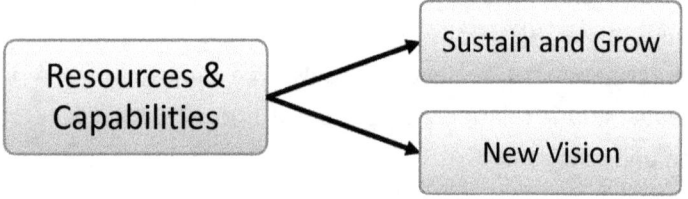

When an organization invests resources and capabilities into achieving a vision and/or mission, they are put at risk. Risk can be regarded as the potential for a resource or capability to suffer damage or loss. For example, the vision to develop the next generation of TV puts reputation and financial resources at risk if the outcome results in a failure.

The most common forms of investment are as follows:

- Financial resources

- Buildings

- Equipment

- Relationships with external parties

- Inventions and innovations

- Processes

- Market share

- Reputation

- Capability of the people

The extent to which an organization can assign resources and capabilities to a new vision will depend on their business model. For example, an organization that develops highly innovative and sought-after products may charge a high price for every unit and generate high profits. Large portions of these profits will be consumed as the organization incurs very high costs associated with the development of the next generation of products.

2. Risk and the probability of success

Risk impacts the probability of success for the overall organizational vision. In particular, risk is associated with the design and strategy associated with achieving the vision as well as the specific implementation plan. As a result, leaders need to be aware of all potential outcomes to their strategy and the associated risks for each one. Each risk will have an associated impact and a probability that it will actually happen. Finally, leaders need to have appropriate contingency plans to address each impact.

Risk ⇨ Impact ⇨ Probability ⇨ Contingency plans

Although there are numerous possible risks to a strategy, we should try to limit the scope to a manageable level and focus on those that are reasonable. Leaders should not take unnecessary risks that could impact an organization's overall health. A risk that has a medium to high probability of causing a business to cease trading should be avoided.

Visions with greater levels of ambition will also carry greater levels of risk. Pushing the boundaries of what an organization is capable of achieving also means moving further and further into the unknown, with associated higher levels of risk.

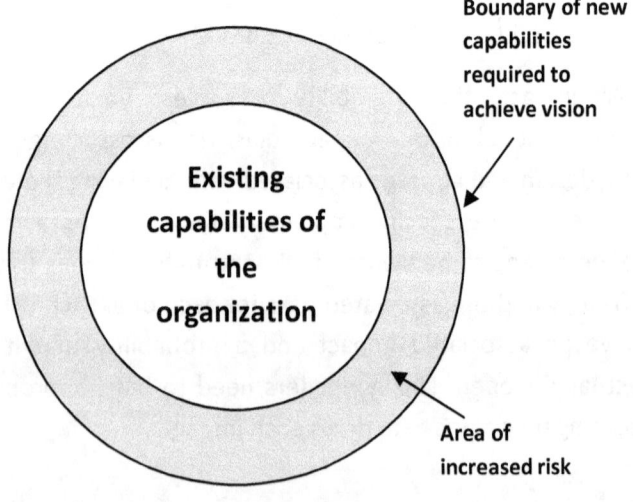

Boundary of new capabilities required to achieve vision

Existing capabilities of the organization

Area of increased risk

Consider an organization that discovers a possible cure for the common cold. They set a vision to develop and sell the drug on a royalty basis to a large pharmaceutical company. We can begin to develop a risk analysis which will enable the leadership team to evaluate and manage risks throughout the life of the vision.

Risk	Impact	Probability	Contingency
Side effects are severe	Drug is not approved	Low	Develop multiple formulas for the drug. Increase clinical tests.
Additional side effects that were not anticipated	Drug is withdrawn	Very Low	Develop multiple formulas for the drug and re-launch. Increase clinical tests.
Product is too costly	Sales are low	Medium	Develop multiple price models and evaluate feasibility for each.
Competitor develops similar product	Sales are lower than expected	Medium	Develop multiple sales forecasts and evaluate feasibility for each.

If a risk actually happens, then the leadership will need to respond promptly and there are a number of options to be considered:

Response	Details
Ignore	Has the potential to add further risk.
Wait and See	In a small number of cases, this approach allows for further information to emerge and allow for a more informed decision on how to respond.
Avoid	If it is possible, then a strategy to avoid the impact of

	the risk should be examined.
Contingency	If the risk was among the list of potential risks that had been previously identified, then the associated contingency plan should be executed.
New strategy	Design and Implementation leaders must be capable of modifying strategies and implementation plans in a dynamic environment and in response to anticipated and unforeseen events.
Abandon	If the impact of the risk is critical, then there is little choice but to abandon the strategy and start again. This is the 'sinking ship' scenario.

As time progresses, greater levels of certainty will emerge and risks will be reduced or eliminated. In the previous example, clinical trials will eventually determine if there will be severe side effects attaching to the drug. Leaders must manage risk on an ongoing basis and should assign a team to evaluate and report on progress.

3.   The value of the benefits

If an organization is prepared to take risks to achieve a new and better state, then the leadership team needs to determine if the effort and risks are actually worth the benefits that they will bring.

In general terms, there is a relationship between the level of risk taken, the impact on the possibility of success and the benefits that will be realized. A strategy that involves high risks will create an expectation that the benefits and rewards will also be high. Clearly a strategy that has high risk and low levels of reward should be re-evaluated.

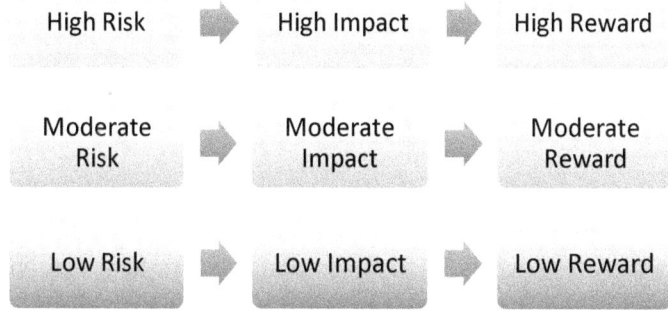

High Risk	→	High Impact	→	High Reward
Moderate Risk	→	Moderate Impact	→	Moderate Reward
Low Risk	→	Low Impact	→	Low Reward

The process of evaluating the 'risk and reward' can cause a leadership to re-evaluate the vision and perhaps revise the scope of what is being targeted. Having a strong risk management process implemented at the beginning of every vision is essential and in its own right can improve the potential for success.

29. Respect

Leaders look for respect. At a personal level, it is the most sought-after accolade for a leader. Leaders aspire to be recognized for their achievements and respected for their wisdom. This will be their legacy.

Wisdom combines knowledge, experience, insight and intelligence and it will take a long time for a person to build a reputation for being wise. Wise people are consulted for their opinion and when these opinions prove to be significantly helpful, their reputation for wisdom increases. Over time, this reputation develops into a state of respect, honour and esteem.

It is important for leaders to understand that respect is earned over time and is not easily acquired. But most of all, respect can be easily lost if a leader brings dishonour on themselves or to the organization. Such dishonour can even result in disgrace or shame.

First let us consider some behaviours that impact a leader's ability to win or lose respect:

Integrity

Leaders build respect by being honourable in what they do and how they do it. Integrity means that a leader will remain faithful to the goal of delivering success for an organization. It suggests that everything they say and do is focused only on a successful outcome. Everything unites in a single direction towards the future state as defined in the vision.

When it comes to behaviours, it primarily means that actions and words are in harmony. Such behaviour enables everyone to trust the leader and it is this trust and confidence that brings respect.

Leaders lose respect when integrity is lost. Tabloid newspapers have almost turned a lack of integrity into an industry. Leaders who ask their organization to behave in one way and fail to behave the same way themselves lose integrity and respect. No leader can ask an organization to take a cut in bonus if they will not take the same cut themselves.

Courage

Leaders who take brave decisions are respected for their courage. Courage in a situation of extreme pressure suggests that a leader is prepared to take a risk to bring an organization forward. What is admirable is that a leader will take the risk knowing that an adverse outcome could significantly damage their own reputation as a leader. By putting the organization ahead of their own personal interests, the leader earns respect.

Courage which has some element of self-sacrifice will earn a leader the highest level of respect. In January 1909 Ernest

Shackleton came within 112 miles of being the first person to reach the South Pole and decided to turn back because he felt that if they continued they would almost certainly die during the return journey. Three years later, Robert Falcon Scott did reach the pole and his team of five men all died on the way back. Scott is honoured more for his bravery and self-sacrifice in truly terrifying conditions.

Passion

Leaders who are passionate about their endeavours earn respect. Their desire to succeed is demonstrated in powerful emotional displays of enthusiasm and self-belief. These displays motivate the organization to continue the journey towards success.

Many political leaders have made passionate speeches during the course of history. In the 20th century many of these speeches were captured on film and video. They are worth watching – if only to get a sense of what passion looks like in real life. Here are a few:

- "Ask not what your country can do for you...". J. F. Kennedy

- "I have a dream...". Martin Luther King

- "We shall fight on the beaches...". Winston Churchill

- "We choose to go to the moon...". J. F. Kennedy

- "This great nation will endure as it has endured...". F. D. Roosevelt

- "But has the last word been said? No." Charles de Gaulle

Interpretation

One outstanding ability that is often found in leaders is their insight. Leaders look at seemingly ordinary events and draw conclusions that most people cannot see. This ability to interpret events in a unique way earns a leader respect.

The interpretation can often be a reassurance to the organization that goals and objectives are reasonable and will be met. It can reinforce the feeling that the organization is in 'safe hands'. Organizations need this reassurance at regular intervals from their leaders.

We are all equal

Leaders can achieve exceptional goals and they deserve the credits they receive. But leaders should not lose sight of their equality as a human amongst humans. To excel in any field of human endeavour does not entitle a person to feel superior to anyone else. This is true for great artists, musicians, writers, and so on, just as it is for leaders.

Leaders who keep a level head and their feet on the ground will earn a significant amount of respect. Equally, leaders who try to put themselves on a pedestal looking down on others will lose respect – rapidly.

Talk to me any time about any thing

Leaders who are approachable and understanding will earn respect. Having a connection with people at all levels in an organization and being willing to interact with everyone can be very powerful in leading an organization.

Leaders who eat lunch in the canteen with everyone else and discuss the ball game or the price of beer. Leaders who have 'away from work' recreational days. Leaders who have breakfast every month with a selection of people across the organization. All these allow the leader to get to know people and allow people to get to know their leader – as individuals.

While 'open door' policies are admirable, that's all they do - open a door. Leaders need to get out and about and make purposeful and meaningful attempts to interact with people. Any attempts to interact with people that are seen as superficial will have a negative impact.

Putting one's own ambitions ahead of the organization's goals

Decisions made by leaders must be made in the interest of the organization's success. To make a decision that is motivated by one's own ambition can significantly damage a leader's respect.

Leaders love success and hate failure. But leaders should not separate the success of the organization from their own personal success. In most cases, the leader's personal ambition for success and that of the organization are one and the same. If a leader's personal ambition is beyond the current capability of the organization then a leader must be willing to be satisfied at what is achievable rather than lead an organization to a potential series of failed goals.

Having an inflated view of their ability

Inasmuch as every human is different to every other human, then every leader is different to every other leader. Any given leader has a unique combination of skills, knowledge and experience. Understanding your capability is essential for every leader. It is just as important to understand your strengths as it is to understand your weaknesses.

Leaders who feel that they do not have all the skills necessary to bring success to an organization will bring additional leadership capabilities through the formation of a leadership team. Leaders should recognise strengths in others and avoid trying to exaggerate their own abilities. Only speak with authority about those things you are authorised to speak about. Let engineers engineer and let leaders lead.

Directing recognition to oneself

Leadership can be a lonely pursuit and it is unlikely that anyone will come along and give you a pat on the back and say 'well done'. In fact, a leader must be the one who spends time patting others on the back.

Let success be recognition in its own right. Offer recognition to others and always avoid trying to direct credit to oneself.

A leader who takes excessive credit is guaranteed to lose respect.

Being supportive of their teams

Leaders must support the people in the organization at all times. A leader guides an organization into the unknown and many people are uncomfortable with the uncertainty that this brings. Offering support eases the uncertainty and brings respect. Leaving people in a situation where they feel alone in taking decisions will certainly damage a leader's ability to build respect.

30. Presence – What happens when I walk into a room?

Leaders project their personality and character by their presence. Presence includes the way a leader speaks and listens as well as body posture and movement. People observe and react to the presence of a leader and this contributes to a position of support or opposition to the vision, design and implementation plans.

A vision may be fundamentally sound and worth pursuing but if it is communicated poorly by a leader who projects a lack of personal conviction or confidence, then the organization's attempts to reach the future state may fail.

In this way, we need to separate the message from the messenger. Or, to be more exact, from the manner in which the messenger delivers the message. People will look at a vision and decide whether to support it based on its own merits. But leaders do not simply distribute their ideas in written documents and emails, they deliver the message personally. People do not follow ideas, they follow leaders with convincing ideas. And leaders use their presence to convince others to follow.

Once people follow a leader, they continually observe the leader and their presence when they walk into a room.

People need to be reassured continuously that the leader still feels the goals are achievable. In many cases, the existence of a significant problem can be observed in the presence of a leader before they even utter a word. Strong presence comes from a person with robust and forthright convictions.

Let us look at two key elements of leadership presence.

Confidence and self-belief

Leaders who are confident speak with composure and assuredness. They respond immediately to questions and body movements suggest they are in control. Their head is raised. Their hands move with sharp and swift gestures. They look people directly in the eye. They prefer to walk across a stage rather than stand at a podium. People remain quiet and listen attentively when they talk.

Passion

Leaders project passion through emotion. Perhaps the emotions that are most visible are courage, determination and anticipation. Body movements include the clenching of fists, the raising of arms, the pointed finger, movements of the eyes as they attempt to look at every person individually.

In contrast, leaders with poor presence can negatively impact on the organization's morale and commitment. Poor presence includes fear and uncertainty and contributes to low confidence. They appear nervous and the flow of their delivery is poor.

Consider a leader who is about to deliver a progress update to the overall leadership team. The message will include details of a significant problem that has been encountered in the days leading up to the meeting. One leader could deliver the message with strong presence and indicate their belief that a solution can be found. Another leader could deliver the message with poor presence and come across as unsure about the outcome. Try to remember that the circumstances are the same; it is simply a question of the leader's presence and how the organization responds.

Every message is capable of being delivered with strong presence or poor presence. It comes down to the leader and their presence of character and personality. It is almost impossible to learn presence. It is something that a person is born with and builds upon.

31. Emotions – the passion and the tears

Leaders do not typically display emotions in a visible way.

Over time we have conditioned leaders to behave with composure at all times and avoid strong outbursts of emotion – whether joyous or sorrowful. Yet the most memorable speeches by leaders are those which have been delivered with passion. Passion comes from a sense of determination and results from emotions of hope and enthusiasm.

Expressions of emotions from leaders can be very powerful. They can significantly influence people's opinion of a leader. They can instil hope or fear.

Expressions of emotion must be appropriate in order to be effective. Expressions of joy and happiness are appropriate and usually come after the organization has had to endure many hardships to reach the future state.

It is reasonable for a leader to express emotions of sadness in difficult circumstances. Such expressions must be coupled with emotions of hope and determination that a brighter, better future will happen.

It is also reasonable for a leader to express emotions of anger when they feel an injustice has occurred. Such expressions should not lead to reprisal injustices on others. Instead, a leader should turn anger into determination and belief that the organization will overcome and move forward towards its goals.

When a leader expresses emotions of fear it is likely that the leader has developed doubts about the organization's future. The leader begins to feel helpless and anxious that they cannot find a solution. They have lost their courage and conviction. Leaders in a state of fear usually step down or are removed. An organization being led by a leader who is fearful may be in danger of not surviving.

It is not possible for a person to change their emotional response to an event or circumstance but outward expressions can be managed and leaders must learn how to manage these expressions appropriately. In particular, extreme outward expressions are typically inappropriate – particularly those of anger and fear.

32. *Leadership integrity*

A leader's primary focus is on achieving organizational success. In addition, many leaders place importance on integrity and see it as an integral part of how they behave and act as role models for everyone in the organization. For most leaders, success can only be declared when the goal has been reached and everyone has behaved with integrity. Leaders pay particular attention to the issue of integrity as it inevitably reflects on the level of respect that they achieve.

Leadership integrity means that a leader will behave in accordance with a set of values, beliefs and expectations that have been set as the standard behavioural norms for the organization as a whole. It also means that a leader behaves in accordance with the law of the country.

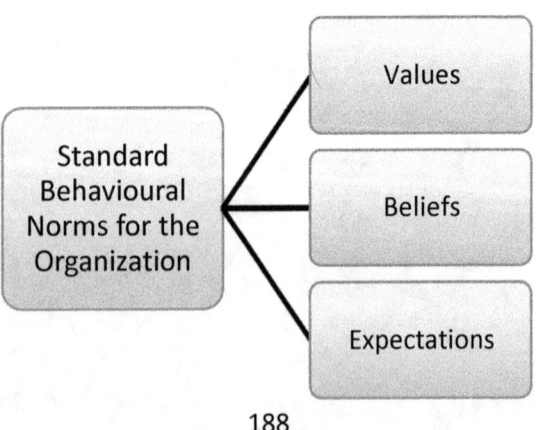

Leaders aim to have complete behavioural alignment across the organization regardless of one's position in the hierarchy of owners, leaders, management or individual contributors.

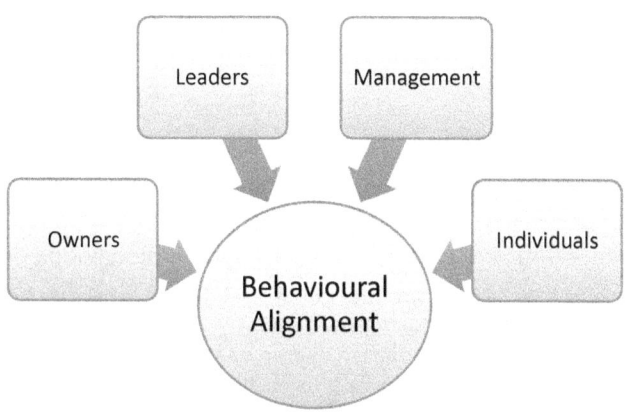

Behavioural norms exist both internally within an organization and outside the organization in society as a whole. Both sets of norms act independently and may be in alignment in some areas and in conflict in others. Leaders may be adhering to the organizational behavioural norms and be seen to be acting with integrity, while at the same time some parts of society may view the same behaviours as being outside the societal behaviour norm and accuse the leaders as having lost integrity.

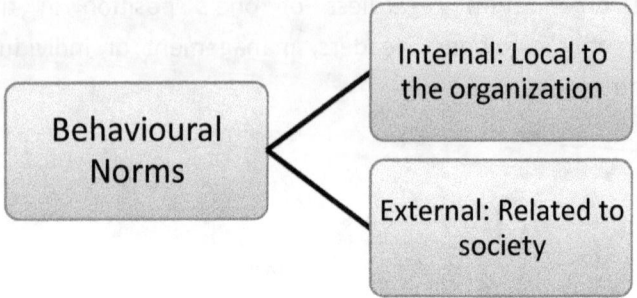

Behavioural Norms

- **Internal: Local to the organization**
- **External: Related to society**

Standard behavioural model

Leaders define the standard of acceptable behaviour in an organization. This can be expressed in an organizational value statement.

If an organization places a value on courtesy between individuals then any behaviour that could be regarded as aggressive would be regarded as outside the norm. Here are some examples of behavioural norms:

- Everyone is expected to tidy their workspace at the end of each day.

- Everyone is expected to recycle disposable items.

- Everyone is expected to maintain confidentiality.

- Everyone is expected to adhere to a dress code.

- Everyone is expected to lend a hand in a time of crisis.

- Everyone is expected to adhere to the code of practice governing travel and entertainment expenses.

The list of behavioural norms could be quite extensive. However, if an organization places value on integrity, then some form of list will be important in creating a standard that can be communicated and that everyone understands.

Behavioural norms can create the impression that perfection is required by all individuals in the way they conduct themselves. As we are all humans, perfection is difficult – particularly in relation to how we behave. Behavioural norms set the level that everyone should aspire to and there will be a need for some flexibility in managing people's behaviour.

For example, a person who is an outstanding contributor may have a real behavioural difficulty in keeping their workplace tidy. Their manager may choose to be flexible in this regard as long as reasonable efforts are made on a frequent basis. By contrast, an outstanding contributor who persistently uses inappropriate language towards colleagues at meetings may have stepped across the line of acceptable behaviour and may need to be disciplined.

Getting every individual in an organization to uphold the behavioural norms can be difficult. But every individual must respect the behavioural norms and make every effort to apply them as they contribute to the organization. Every individual is also required to take personal responsibility for their own behaviour.

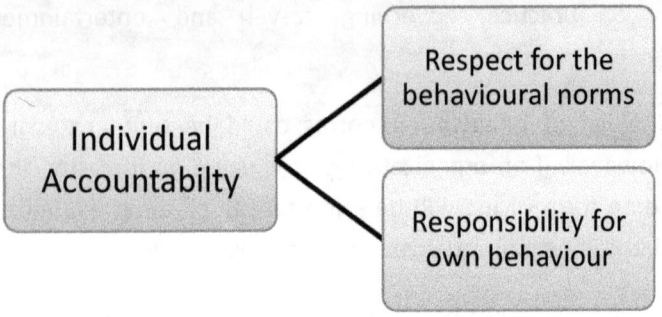

If an organization fails to explicitly state what the behavioural norm is for any given situation, then one will emerge over time. It will typically emerge by way of example set by the leadership. In this way, an organization can have explicit and implied behavioural norms.

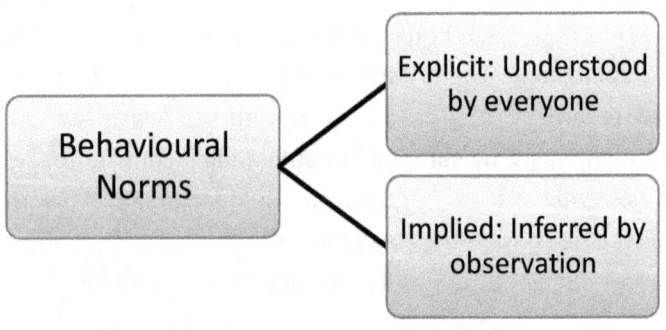

Once again, leaders are the role model for all behavioural norms but are particularly responsible for acting as the benchmark for implied behavioural norms.

Trust and loyalty

Trust plays a central role in integrity. It is not reasonable or practical to monitor and police people's behaviour at all times. Everyone is trusted to remain loyal to the behavioural norms. Since the standard of behavioural norms is the same for everyone, leaders are not exempt from what is regarded as acceptable behaviour; in fact, leaders should be role models for the standard they have defined. This can be challenging for leaders and there is likely to be less flexibility and understanding if a leader behaves outside the organizational norm.

When change happens

Organizational change can lead to a change in the behavioural norm. Since organizational change occurs with relative frequency, it is the responsibility of the leadership to reinforce the behavioural norms. What was acceptable last year may not be acceptable today and could be very different next year.

Consider the example of an organization that has no explicit behavioural norm for how individuals spend money on entertainment. Since profits are good, controls are not rigidly managed or enforced. People use their discretion and follow examples set by senior managers and organizational leaders. Suddenly, profits decline and the organization needs to set new standards. Entertainment costs are subject to guidelines and everyone is asked to apply them.

Leaders must be the first to advocate and practice any changes to behavioural norms.

When a leader falls from grace

When a leader behaves outside the behavioural norm it can lead to a loss of integrity. Depending on the gravity of the transgression, the impact can vary from a minor loss of respect to the resignation of the leader. Extreme loss of personal integrity has even resulted in indictments for criminal behaviour in society.

Every time a leader is seen to act without integrity it will result in some loss of respect. A loss of respect leads to a lack of trust and no matter how small this is, it can be very difficult to recover. When an organization loses its ability to trust the leadership, morale is affected and the impact on an organization's drive for success can be significant.

Loss of Integrity → Loss of Respect → Loss of Trust

Let us look at a set of sample situations where a loss of leadership integrity might occur:

Behavioural Norm	Transgression	Degree of Integrity Loss
Appropriate use of organization's infrastructure including phones, computers, etc.	Excessive use of the photocopier for personal use	Minor
Adherence to guidelines for moderate and reasonable expenditure on entertainment	Excessive indulgence in very expensive meals at very expensive restaurants	Moderate
In a time of significant cost management, everyone is asked to take a reduction to their remuneration	To accept large increases to a remuneration package including pay, share options and bonuses as outlined in an original contract of employment	High
To report on the organization's activities in an honest and truthful manner	To misrepresent the financial statements of the organization	Extreme

Does integrity matter?

Yes. It matters a great deal to an organization.

A leader is the living persona of an organization and how a leader behaves is integral to how the organization is perceived – both internally and externally.

Think of the leader of an organization that you know. Perhaps a business, a hospital, a sports club, a government, a charity. Do you think you are influenced by the way the leader behaves? If we admire a leader, then we are likely to support the organization and if we disapprove of the leader's behaviour, then we are likely to avoid interaction with the organization.

If we see a leader promising to deliver new features to a product and it does not happen, then we begin to lose trust and confidence in the leader *and* the organization. Sales fall away as expectations are not met.

Integrity means there is 'wholeness and consistency' to everything the leader says and does. This creates trust and confidence and unless a situation of extremely unusual circumstances occurs, a leader must be honourable.

33. *Heroism*

Leaders are heroes because the commitment required of them causes some aspect of themselves or their life to be sacrificed. Heroism is not dependent on whether the goal is achieved or not. Leaders become heroes in the process of reaching the future state and most heroism is associated with Implementation leaders.

Leaders become heroes because of their actions. We characterize these actions in terms of bravery and courage in the face of adversity.

Heroes become heroes only because they lead an organization into the unknown. A heroic leader looks into the future and tries to determine the appropriate actions that will lead to success. They use their knowledge, intellect, intuition and judgement to the highest level of their ability to evaluate all possible paths forward and to identify the one path that leads to success.

Heroic leaders behave according to their beliefs and values. If they value the people in their organization, they are prepared to do anything and everything to support them. If they believe that a cure for a disease can be found, they will sacrifice a great deal of their time and energy in the pursuit of a solution. Organizations have inbuilt belief and value systems and it is typical for a heroic leader to be their primary advocate. Their actions and behaviours demonstrate the worthiness of the organization's endeavours.

Leaders can take an exceptional burden on themselves in order to bring the organization forward. This includes going beyond the scope of their own responsibilities and taking on the responsibilities of others. It involves the taking of exceptional risks which have the potential to significantly advance the organization's progress. These 'make or break' situations occur frequently along the journey towards the vision.

Heroic leaders are inspirational and motivate the rest of the organization to behave according to a set of values and principles. Their behaviour often positions them as role models for exceptional performance. When challenges arise, they immediately take an active part in trying to find a solution. They are the first to volunteer. They may not have the skills to bring about a solution but they offer support merely by being present with those who can find the answers. They are willing to carry out any task in order to make progress. They make the coffee, drive a delivery truck, post the mail – whatever it takes to get the job done.

Heroic leaders are enablers. They rarely work alone and ask the organization to follow in their footsteps. They redeploy resources and capabilities in a way in which they feel the outcome is more certain. They think rapidly and issue instructions with certainty and confidence. They identify weaknesses and eliminate them.

True heroes do what they do for the honour and glory of the organization and not for any credit that might accrue to them personally. They are humble and tend to draw attention to the heroism of those who follow rather than those who lead. There can be as much heroism in a team who follows a leader into the unknown as there is in the leader themselves.

Heroic leaders take calculated risks with moderate to high levels of peril. A situation with a low level of risk is usually mundane and does not warrant any heroism. A situation with an extremely high level of risk is unlikely to be achieved and has the potential to damage or over-consume resources.

Leaders who take excessive risks to themselves and the organization may not be regarded as heroes. There can be a thin line between heroism and foolish endeavour.

Heroic leaders can make personal sacrifices in different ways. Entrepreneurial innovators may not have sufficient funds and resources to turn their ideas into a commercial success. So they sacrifice their quality and standard of life in order to put all available resources towards the successful achievement of their goal. In many cases, they do not become materially wealthy people and wealth is only acquired by subsequent generations of the family.

Leaders sacrifice a great deal of their time in the pursuit of their goals. While most people think in terms of a finite working week of say 40 hours, leaders work at every waking moment. They constantly review strategies and plans and apply innovation to solving emerging problems. These activities cannot be time-boxed into a standard working day.

In some situations a leader knows that a personal sacrifice is the only way to achieve success. They continue with their actions knowing that they need to become a martyr in order for the organization to reach its goal. Martyrdom is the ultimate form of heroic leadership and although we tend to think about it in terms of political and military endeavours, it can occur in many areas of society including business, human rights, science, education and so on.

34. When it's time to step aside

Leaders have tenure. Leaders emerge, deliver results through periods of organizational development and, eventually, leaders stand aside.

Most Leaders have a period in their life in which they reach their maximum performance. There are no set rules about this – either in terms of when it happens or for how long it will last. Many leaders reach their peak ability quite early in their life and remain effective for many, many years. Given that a significant part of a leader's capability has its origins in their character and personality, it is reasonable to see leaders perform from an early age.

All leaders will continue to develop their ability through the acquisition of knowledge and by experiencing leadership at first hand. However, leadership demands a lot from a person and the dynamics of change in an organization will gradually bring some level of obsolesce to a leader's style of vision.

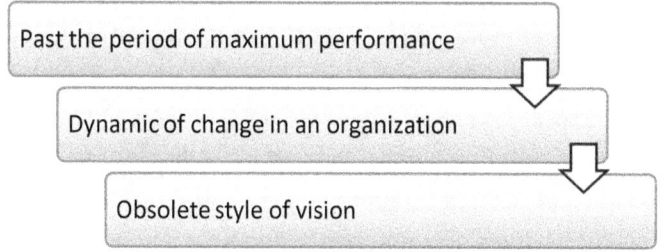

Leaders who step down in one organization can potentially take up a leadership role in another organization who are at a different point in their evolution. This happens – a lot. Even leaders who retire can continue to make significant contributions in a consultative way. Such leaders can be extremely beneficial because of their extensive knowledge and experience.

The time at which a leader steps down can be determined by the organizational rules and regulations. For example, many countries will only allow a president/prime minister to have up to two tenures in power. Shareholders of a business typically re-elect the board on an annual basis.

I am getting results. Why shouldn't I stay?

You might think that as long as a leader is getting results they should remain in their position. For many organizations, this can be the normal practice and leaders *should* remain in place as long as the results are good.

However, leaders should watch for early signs that their style of vision is no longer a fit for the organization. Organizations evolve and change direction, perhaps because the shareholders, owners, trustees or electorate decide that a change is necessary. Just because a particular approach is working today does not mean that it will work indefinitely. Leaders may find it difficult to adapt their style to the new direction and may struggle to deliver effective leadership in the new era. For example, a leader may have been very effective at leading the organization to create a series of products and sell them effectively through a chain of retail outlets. In contrast, they may struggle to provide leadership if the organization begins to sell their products through the Internet. Perhaps the leader is more comfortable in developing relationships with managers of retail outlets and may not possess an adequate understanding of the technology that supports internet-based business. They soon become uncomfortable and begin to show signs of low confidence. When these signs become visible, they should consider stepping down.

Ignoring the signs that the end is in sight

Leaders who ignore the early signs that their tenure is reaching an end are taking significant risks. Some leaders persevere in the hope that they can still provide leadership in the new circumstances; they try hard to adjust their style. But things can go wrong:

- The organizational results are impacted.

- People begin to lose confidence in the leadership and uncertainty sets in.

- Incorrect decisions are made.

- Potential successors position themselves to take over.

- Support for the leader begins to decrease and an underground political alliance emerges.

- Conflict begins between individuals on the leadership team.

If a leader remains in power then the situation may reach a climax. Organizational results become so bad that the viability of the organization is now in question. Typically, the leader will be removed.

Although this seems quite dramatic, we should not underestimate the pace at which a situation of instability can develop. A leader who was once a hero can easily become a villain.

Developing a successor

All leaders are obliged to develop a successor and every organization should have a succession management process which identifies all potential future leaders for the organization. Developing successors is essential to the continuity of the organization and is critical in a situation where a leader departs. An organization cannot afford to lose momentum when a leader departs.

Leaders may not be the right people to <u>choose</u> their successors unless they are capable of being totally objective. There is a risk that they may gravitate towards individuals who share a similar leadership style and organizational vision. There are situations where it will be appropriate for a new leader to continue with the current direction and approach, but it also possible that an entirely fresh approach will be required which demands a very different type of leader.

In contrast, leaders can play a vital role in developing the skills and capabilities of the next generation of leaders.

At the organizational leadership level, there are two areas of focus:

1.	• The selection of an organizational leader
2.	• The selection of the organizational leadership team

The owners, trustees, shareholders, council (or similar) will select the Organizational leader. The members of the organizational leadership team should have some input on the candidates, including their own candidature.

The Organizational leader will choose the members of the organizational leadership team. Any member of the organization should be able to put forward their credentials for selection. Managers and individual contributors should be given equal consideration.

Leaders have two roles in developing potential successors for their own role:

1.	• Be a Coach to a 'Ready Now' candidate
2.	• Be a Mentor to a 'Ready Later' candidate

Let's take a brief look at the difference between coaching and mentoring. For the purpose of completeness, I am also including some additional definitions.

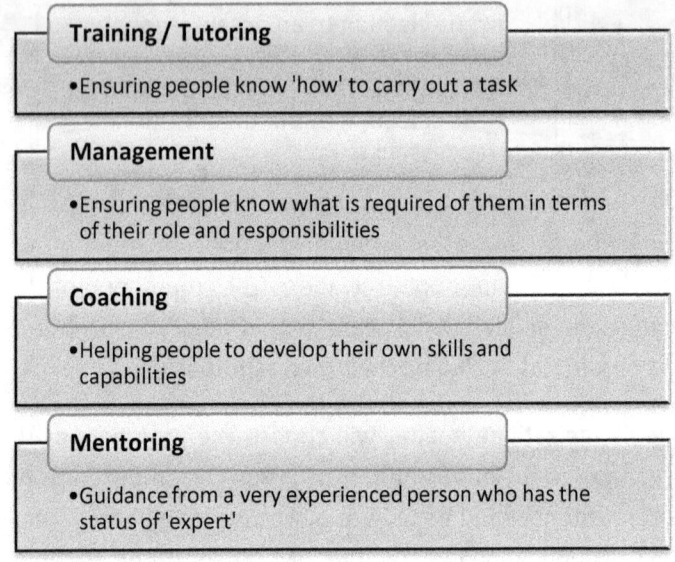

Training / Tutoring
- Ensuring people know 'how' to carry out a task

Management
- Ensuring people know what is required of them in terms of their role and responsibilities

Coaching
- Helping people to develop their own skills and capabilities

Mentoring
- Guidance from a very experienced person who has the status of 'expert'

As a rule, people should only mentor a person where they have no direct reporting relationship. Mentoring is best carried out by experienced leaders who are not directly involved in the day-to-day work of the protégé.

Coaching can be carried out by any person who has extensive leadership experience. The coach is focused on the development of existing skills and capabilities and typically offers advice in specific real-time situations.

'Ready Now' Candidate	'Ready Later' Candidate
• Reports to the current leader • Has demonstrated ability to step up one level in the hierarchy	• Has demonstrated ability to be a leader after a period of continued development and experience

Coaching and mentoring take place over long periods of time, with a typical minimum of six months.

Agreeing the terms of reference and scope of a mentoring programme at the start will go a long way to helping each party get the most from the experience:

- Agree what the protégé expects to achieve and review progress at the end of every second month.

- Try to meet every two weeks for at least an hour.

- Try to meet at a location that is not usual. Consider a room in a different building or rent a room at an office facilities provider.

- Share experiences

- Keep everything confidential.

- Agree on honesty, openness and fairness.

- Try to focus on behaviours and attitudes – not what is right and what is wrong.

- Get to know each other on a personal level and talk about pastimes, favourite sports, and so on.

35. *Bringing it all together*

We can summarize everything about leadership in the following framework:

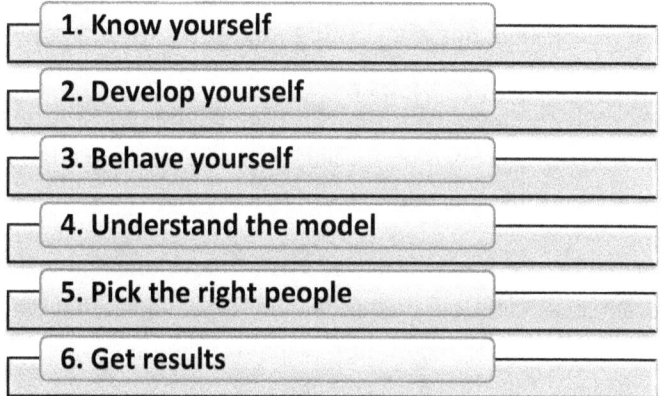

1. Know yourself
2. Develop yourself
3. Behave yourself
4. Understand the model
5. Pick the right people
6. Get results

1. Know yourself

Having a clear profile of your character, personality and intellectual capability is fundamental to being a successful leader.

This profile helps you understand the type of leader you are and will guide you to work in a position in which you have the greatest probability of being successful.

You will understand more about your strengths and weaknesses and from this you can pick a team that has the optimum balance of skills which are necessary to lead an organization forward.

You can use a variety of methods to get a clearer picture of yourself. Do some personality profiles. Confide with close associates and get their feedback. Get a mentor.

2. Develop yourself

Being a leader is not a state that you arrive at. It is a life-long endeavour to develop your skills and capabilities. Constantly re-assess your skills and capabilities and educate yourself on an ongoing basis. Finishing your academic education is only the beginning of this process.

Your talent as a leader is derived from your personality and character as well as the skills and capabilities that you develop over time. Experience in the frontline of leadership significantly adds to your capability.

Read books. Attend courses. Get a coach. Be part of a leadership team. All of these will help you develop yourself. Try to focus on the capabilities that make leaders successful: Inspiration, intuition, judgement, confidence, influence and innovation. Observe other leaders and learn from their approaches. Try to see what works and what does not.

3. Behave yourself

Your behaviour as a leader plays a key part in how you lead an organization to success. Behaviour is central to your interactions with people and these interactions will ultimately decide whether people will support you or not.

Your behaviour is the outward expression of your emotional state. So if you are passionate about achieving the vision of a better future state, this will visible to all in many aspects of your behaviour.

Your behaviour has the potential to attract others to join your organization. It can motivate and inspire people to perform to the maximum extent of their capabilities. It can influence people to support you and offer direct and indirect assistance.

Managing your behaviour allows you to maximize the outcome of every interaction. It can help you to avoid alienating people who may be sensitive to one of your natural behavioural tendencies. In this way, you can develop relationships with everyone who is key to the success of the organization.

4. Understand the model

Leaders should have a model which shapes their approach to leading an organization. A model helps focus your attention on what is important and how you will strive to be successful.

There are many models for leading an organization. It is not a matter of which is right and which is wrong. It is really about using the model that works for you and the organization.

In this book I have outlined a model which has three components:

- The vision of a better state for an organization

- The design of a strategy to bring the organization forward

- The implementation of the strategy using high-performance teams.

This model clearly sets out how an organization can develop and survive over time. It puts creativity and innovation at the centre of an organization's ability to reach a future state that represents progress and advancement. It outlines the role of the leader and helps you build a leadership team which has the right balance of capabilities. It focuses on character, personality, behaviours, intellect and experience as key components of leadership capability.

5. <u>Pick the right people</u>

Leaders very rarely work alone. They need others to help them achieve success for the organization. They select people whom they feel have the necessary resources and capabilities to bring the organization forward. They combine resources, capabilities and processes to create a unique organizational potential to reach a future, better state.

Leaders choose to work with people who can provide much-needed resources in the form of investment, endorsement and introductions to other key people. In this way, leaders use all their powers of influence and persuasion to garner support for their venture.

Leaders select people to work in the organization itself. They outline the vision and inspire others to follow. They motivate people to achieve success, both for themselves and the organization. They reward people for their performance.

Leaders select other leaders to be part of a leadership team. Together, they have the right balance of leadership skills necessary to bring the organization forward. They work together in harmony and use all their energy, creativity and commitment to overcome obstacles and reach the future state.

6.   Get results

In the end, a leader must be successful. Success comes when you reach the future state and after a reasonable period of time has passed, it is clear that the organization has advanced and developed.

The organization has enough resources and capabilities to survive and develop further. It has created a new position for itself in which it has the ability to build additional assets. Everyone feels a sense of achievement and reward.

In the course of being successful, a leader acquires a sense of wisdom about what works and what doesn't. This adds to their overall leadership capability and positions them to take further leadership roles.

When a leader sets out to lead an organization, they focus on results. Right results. Results that represent progress.

Nothing else matters.

www.ingramcontent.com/pod-product-compliance
Lightning Source LLC
Chambersburg PA
CBHW051453170526
45166CB00001B/234